PRAISE FOR *OLD MAN RIDER*

"With glorious, unapologetic brutality, *Old Man Rider* tells, through several vivid vignettes, of Bishop Rider's exploits. Woven in are elements of his humanity, as well as his motivation. Johnson provides a well-written, thoughtful book of revenge, glorious bloody revenge. I found it utterly delightful and want more more more."

—Shannon Kirk, author of *Gretchen*

"Beau Johnson pulls no punches in this final installment of Bishop Rider stories. And rest assured, no one will be spared or saved. Riveting, heartbreaking, and bloody as ever. This collection took a 2x4 to my head—in the best way."

—Curtis Ippolito, author of *Burying the Newspaper Man*

"Johnson's the kind of writer you let drag you across the broken glass screaming because you know the destination's going to make it all worth it. Brutal, dark, unflinching—this is a hell of a Rider story."

—Angel Luis Colon, author of *Hell Chose Me*

"*Old Man Rider* is flat-out amazing. While many of the stories are quick jabs to the gut or punches to the face, they string together in such perfect combinations that the book is an absolute slugfest. Great, wonderful stuff."

—Steve Weddle, author of *Country Hardball*

"Beau Johnson writes the kind of fiction your mother warned you about—feel the trauma, smell the flesh, taste the concrete—*Old Man Rider* is about to stomp you into oblivion."
—Zachary Ashford, author of *When the Cicadas Stop Singing*

"Absorbing and devastating, these are miniature morality plays. As if the angel of death was descending each level of hell, punishing the most evil people in the world. Bishop Rider books are an unapologetic fistful of concrete to the face."
—Manny Torres, author of *Dead Dogs* and *Father Was a Rat King*

"It's said that 'You eat the world or the world eats you.' This theme is (re)introduced early and carried through this last install-ment of Bishop Rider's story. Short, sharp stories delivering Rider's signature violent revenge written with prose like a punch to the face. This cycle might be ended for now, but the work? The work is being done. Highly recommended."
—Alan Baxter, author of *The Gulp* and *Shallow Bend*

"Forget Dirty Harry and The Punisher. Step aside, too, Old Man Logan—there's a new surly old cuss who's the best there is at what he does, and what he does isn't very nice. *Old Man Rider* is a tough, vicious, violent, mean ol' SOB, and Johnson's writing is as dark, brutal, and twisted as ever. Beau's saved the best for last, and these final stories in the life of Bishop Rider are a full-fledged assault upon the reader. I wouldn't expect anything less, and I certainly wouldn't have it any other way."
—Michael Patrick Hicks, author of *Friday Night Massacre*

OLD MAN RIDER

BOOKS BY BEAU JOHNSON

A Better Kind of Hate
The Big Machine Eats
All of Them to Burn
Brand New Dark
Old Man Rider

BEAU JOHNSON

OLD MAN RIDER

A Bishop Rider Book

Down & Out Books
3959 Van Dyke Road, Suite 265
Lutz, FL 33558
DownAndOutBooks.com

Cover design by Wayne Fenlon

ISBN: 1-64396-275-2
ISBN-13: 978-1-64396-275-7

For you. Yes, you.
Christ I love you.

TABLE OF CONTENTS

PREFACE

Well, now this is REALLY awkward. I mean, I said this writing thing of mine was over two books ago, didn't I? You know, after I killed Bishop Rider. Part of the journey is the end, remember? Yeah, about that. Seems something happens when I'm editing books. Seems a certain angry fictional piece of my mind decides it's time to speak up. Anyway, this IS it. For all the marbles, as it were. No take backs. And I did want to make it to an even hundred stories to close out Bishop's struggle, but alas, ninety-five will have to do. These twenty-five new tales connecting and delving into the past, the future, and many a "dirtbag" between. They involve Alex the Betrayer, the man who gives Rider up to Mapone and the reason soccer is now a viewing pleasure and no longer a playable one. John Batista joins us as well, Bishop's partner from his time upon the CCPD. There is also Ray, a man from Rider's tour in Kuwait and builder of "toys" that may or may not go bump in the night. This leaves Jeramiah, the son of Marcel Abrum and the man who started it all—the man who put into motion the demise of a certain mother and sister. Jeramiah's life now dedicated to atoning for what his father and uncle chose to do all those years ago. It's been fun, it's been difficult, but as I have said before: I would never trade it. Not ever. What happens/happened next?

These are their stories.

THE RETURN

It's a year and a half later when Alex decides he's well enough and makes his way back to me. I'd kept tabs, sure, but doing what Alex himself had been participating in for years, I could only take things so far.

Hood up, in dark jeans and dirty sneakers, he and his new walk are coming off the last stair to a basement that wasn't really a basement at all when I pull Kavanaugh up by the hair and tell him not to go anywhere. Kavanaugh, an entirely different story, moans, somehow thinking I actually wanted an answer.

"Some new machinery, I see." He's angry, but to his credit, Alex tries his best to contain it. Could I blame him? For some of it, yes. But not for all of it. If anything, I had to give him that.

"Ray's been busy," I say, wiping my hands and moving to a table each of us knew well. Upon it lay a variety of hammers and hatchets and, leaning against the wall, a chainsaw Alex had always been partial to. We're pre-Jeramiah here, pre-Batista losing parts of his face.

I sit. Alex joins me.

And like that, we get to the bones of it.

Was it right? Me leaving him in the street like that? I have to say yes, and not only because I'd do it the exact same way if I had to, but because I'd warned Alex of the possibility presenting itself. Alex, he doesn't recall this. Not at first. Nor later. He pretends to, certainly, and my kicking foot eventually becomes the cost, but here now, it's not even him getting hit by that car he's on about.

"One time," he says, his hand up and into hair begging for a wash. His hoodie remained, however, and as if he knew what I was thinking, he pulls the material down until his entire forehead is gone. "You think you could have visited me one time. I was in that hospital for months, Bishop. Months!" He kicks back into his chair, more exasperated than petulant. But this here, Alex's attitude, it wasn't new. He'd never been able to see anyone's plight but his own. Him helping us out as he had or not.

All told, it was the very thing Batista had seen from the start.

Unfortunately for me, my right leg especially, I remained blind.

"This is the discussion you want to have? This is you making a case?" I go on, diving deep into things I felt he should have already known; that I did, in fact, want to see how he'd been doing, that I believed he deserved as much. But the work, it wouldn't be jeopardized, not for anyone—myself included. "And when you move back into your mother's house, you feel I should have just, what, dropped on by? Say I was a friend from work?" Arms crossed at the chest, he's pouting openly now, but I wasn't done. Not when I knew he understood. It wasn't how it worked, not in the type of world we lived in. And then I find myself thinking back to that night, to those Bethune boys and how they slaughtered that family, saving the youngest Acosta boy for last. How Alex and I go in to take care of things and how, as it sometimes happens, things go pear-shaped in the blink of an eye. Ending not only with the younger Bethune behind the wheel of his Camaro and Alex meeting the metal it's made of firsthand, but that he comes back down to the blacktop at such an angle I hardly believe he survived.

On his back, looking to me from eyes that bled, I hold his hand as he begs for me to stay. I can not comply, however. Doing what I knew I would if the situation ever came to be.

Sirens approaching, I leave him. I abandon him.

I do what needs to be done.

"You can't even apologize?"

I stop. I breathe. I try to accept he has never had as much skin in the game as me. It doesn't work. Not as I hoped.

"I won't, Alex. And I think you knew this before it even entered your mind to come here. This here, it's everything you signed on for. I never presented it as anything more. Leave now, I call it a wash, each of us doing a bit of good in the process. You choose to stay, however, this ends now. Right here. You can't have it both ways."

I wait. Watch as he pushes his tongue into the back part of his top lip. Coming forward, arms up in the table, he says, "If I agree, what are the chances I get to help you with buddy over there?"

Over my shoulder, I look to Kavanaugh, the man hogtied and leaking from more than a few places. Straining, he's in the blue pajama bottoms I found him in, the veins at his temples and upon his neck up and out like steel.

"Depends," I say.

"On what?"

"On whether or not you've forgotten how a pair of pliers can become a man's best friend." He smiles at that, and for a moment, things are almost as they'd been before Bethune hit him with that car. Not perfect, no, but manageable.

I'm wrong, of course, and hindsight would come to do what it has always done best. But this time, it wouldn't just fuck me in the ass. No, this time it would make me bleed.

Kavanaugh, however, he becomes a tether of sorts—a pastime that brings Alex back into the fold. Not a perfect truth, no, as none of us can ever know a man's true heart, but I felt what we'd been through, the people we'd saved, it could mend what he felt had been broken.

Wrong. So goddamn wrong.

But the future that awaited me, the one where Alex eventually sells me out to a shitbird by the name of Mapone, it was just that: the future. The two of us still very much within the here and now.

"Kavanaugh here, he likes children," I tell Alex as we approach the man, each of us stepping to either side. "Liked them so much he felt the need to bury them alive once he was done with them. Isn't that right, Brett?" The old man looks up to me as best he can, his mouth and gag a curtain of semi-dried blood. "Thirty-four years in Millhaven, though, it can sometimes give a man a belief he may have paid for his crimes. Before you came in, I was about to explain to Brett how certain people tend to get this part wrong."

"I take it you have something special in mind?"

He knew me well. Wasn't always I drew up a plan either, but sometimes? Sometimes I wanted to see it dawn in their eyes before we took them apart.

Was it fair? I thought so. But then again, I'd never asked.

Even before Alex began descending the stairs, I'd taken the last of Kavanaugh's teeth. Pliers in hand, Alex continues on from where I'd left off, going to work on the man's fingernails. The muffled screams that arise from this come large at first and then fall nonexistent as Kavanaugh passes out. When he wakes, we're out back of the Buchannan house. It's dusk, and the heart of Culver is to the left of us, as wounded as she'd ever been.

Shovels at our sides, we stand there, Alex on one side, me on the other.

Behind one-inch plexiglass, Kavanaugh lay unbound and ungagged, the man now looking up to us from what would be his final resting place. I watch as he puts the pieces together, realizing the coffin for what it is.

"You have air, Kavanaugh. You also have water and food. Use it or not, I don't care. Unlike those girls, the choice will never not be yours." True. All of it. The special-request casket and pumped-in O_2 courtesy of Ray. The twenty-four bottles of water and sixteen power bars lining the walls of said casket, well, that was all me. Wanted the man to have enough time to ponder his situation before the inevitable took hold. Seemed more than fair once you weighed it against the things that brought him to my attention in the first place. Isn't until the man starts to head-butt the plexiglass and his nail-less fingers begin to smear blood that Alex and I start in on the dirt. Muffled as they were, we receive screams in return, but not just any old screams. What erupts from Kavanaugh is primal, from down deep, and awash in a terror not many men experience.

His victims, however, they still deserved more.

It's full dark by the time we finish. Alex leans his shovel against the house, lights another smoke, and then looks down toward Culver. Lit up as it was, it could almost pass for sane. Like the world over, nothing could be further from the truth.

"You think he saw you coming?" Alex asks, hooking a thumb back toward the flattened earth. "Not physical-like, but that somebody coulda been looking for payback?"

I didn't know. Nor did I care. Not like most people would. But Alex's question, it was a blind spot for me. My obsession, as ever, blotting out the sun.

"Men like Kavanaugh, I put nothing past them," I say. "We do, it gives them an advantage. I see nothing good coming from that."

Alex turns to me then, his hoodie's default position already up and back in place. "I think I like it when it happens that way. When they don't know. I think it may be my favorite part."

He leaves me then, and as I gather the shovels, you'd think I might have stopped to consider his words. I don't, though. Not once. And to this day, the blame rests exactly where it should. I'm not saying I like this fact, only that it's there. It doesn't change things, either. Not in the end. In the end, Alex would scream just as much as Kavanaugh did.

If memory serves, perhaps a little more.

EAT THE WORLD

I catch most men unaware and by design. And by design, I mean Ray.

You eat the world, or the world eats you.

He wasn't the first man to say this, nor would he be the last. I look to him then, there in the past, the both of us out behind the Buchannan house. It's early but already hot and not a cloud between the two. Beyond us lay Culver, down and out front of the valley. Filled with more atrocities than most cities believe existed, it's been my home since before I take off the shield and come back from the very same war that entwined my life with Ray's.

"Three months until he's released. Is it doable? Those are the questions. I get that." Ray stands at the corner of the safehouse, alternately looking down one side of it and back to the other. He retains his head at this point in time, and just a hint of grey had begun to sneak into the stuff above his ears.

His head he loses to a madman named Hightower. Hightower lobbing it to me from the balcony of a defunct motel on a Sunday afternoon. I eventually get my hands on this man and, in the same basement I now stood above, take the better part of a year to dismantle him. But still, the damage remained unrepairable, and my friend would leave this world in a way that never should have been.

But here, now, such actions had yet to occur.

Here, now, we are pre-Jeramiah, pre-Alex betraying me to Mapone, and pre-Ray and the machetes set to take him apart.

"Well, is it?" He doesn't answer me, not right away, the man in a type of thought process I'd seen before. I wait. I watch. I see his aversion to socks has lived to fight another day.

"He won't be able to break the plexiglass, not at a thickness of one inch and not within the space we limit him to. That's not my concern. The amount of carbon monoxide he'll be creating is what worries me. Will I be able to pull enough of it out while pumping oxygen in?"

I wanted to bury a man named Kavanaugh alive. That was the deal. Wanted him to know what it felt like to have done to him what he'd done to too many others, him serving thirty years for his crimes or not.

In the end, Ray ends up doing what he always did best and made it work. The final product consisting of separate generators and twin runners that ran up under the bottom of the coffin, extracting and releasing gases in equal measure.

Before I leave him, though, I receive a call. It's Batista. And there's something in the big man's voice, something I hadn't heard before. He'd found him, he says. He *had* him.

Who, I say.

"Gank," he replies. "I fucking found Gank."

And just like that: time to go to work.

Rudy Gank had been the beginning, but his piece-of-shit brother Henry became the end. Serial killers, they took eighteen girls from the world by the time everything is said and done. In part because we'd thought it was over the moment I removed Rudy Gank from the board, the battery cables I'd hooked to the older brother's scrotum a smoky, charred mess by the time we parted ways. But it wasn't over, not when other girls began to turn up, pieces of family pets caught in their intestinal tracts as well.

"It's happening again," Batista says. And then, once we'd pieced things together, "How the hell do we miss him having a brother?"

"It happens," I remind him, and go one step further and reiterate we hadn't caught on to the first brother fast enough because of the business he'd inherited from an uncle who held a different last name.

It didn't matter. Any of it. All of it taking a toll on Batista and whittling the detective down through the years—bit by bit and murder after murder. Ineffectiveness and empathy, it will do this to a cop. Sadly, it also forms to create the worst type of fuse.

Hence my reservations about the big man's voice and my eventual race to the Ronson house.

"No...stop...too deep." And it was, the piece of rebar Batista had up into the man's anus almost to the detective's wrist. The smell assaults me, permeating the room, and I watch Batista's shoulders dip when he hears me come off the last stair. "I tried, Rider. I thought I could."

He'd get there eventually, but at this point in time, my brand of justice remained a bone of contention between us, old and gnawed on by years.

I approach them both, Gank already halfway to broken, his face pressed hard against the cement wall. I lay a hand to the forearm not against the back of Gank's skull, and just like that, John relinquishes the steel.

Only when he closes the door at the top of the basement stairs do I turn and face a man whose face was so much like one I thought I'd never see again. Small eyes below thick eyebrows stare back at me, and a mustache that wasn't really a mustache at all sat layered in tears and blood. With his jeans and underwear around his ankles, he slides away from me, a trail of blood and shit following him like a snake.

I hunker down.

I speak.

Tell him how his brother screamed when I ripped apart his eyes.

In turn, he tells me why they did it—that even dirty bitches needed to eat.

It brings the hammer into play, and with it I unhinge the right side of the man's jaw with the second of three swings. Done, I move to the middle of the room and remove a lid that led to a septic tank that had absolutely nothing to do with anything even remotely close to what it'd been constructed for. Two feet by two feet, it couldn't hold Gank, not at the dimensions he was. I knew this, of course, and it's why the chainsaw already hung in my hand.

You eat the world, or the world eats you.

I'm not the first man to say this, nor would I be the last. What I'll add is this:

Burn them all.

OF MEMORIES AND MAPONE

The moment the axe goes through my right foot and into the wood floor, I find myself back in Mapone's office. Behind his desk, Mapone is there, the empty caverns of his eyes as deep as I remember.

"Long time, Rider," he says, and to the man's credit, he *is* looking my way. A little down and to the left, sure, but hey, what's a no-eyed excuse for a human being going to do?

Beside him stands the skinhead who holds the axe, the one who takes my leg that day. On either side of the chair I'm bound to are the other two men who round out our fivesome. Both are shaved to the wood like Axe-man, both in beater T's and rolled-up jeans.

More is said. Tons. But it seems to happen faster when I look back. Trick of the mind? Shock? Perhaps a mixture of the two. Regardless, it happens. Axe-man jumping the gun before Mapone gives the actual order, and then for me it's a combination of unrelenting pain and goodbye treadmills. Leaving me to understand that life hadn't only chosen to fuck me to the point of climax once more, but that she'd decided to forgo any type of lube.

Enter the trade-off I never knew I had coming.

One of the skinheads, the one to my left, he isn't a skinhead. Shorter than the other two, his name is Jeramiah Abrum, and although I didn't know it at the time, we were connected in ways that amaze me still.

Jeramiah Abrum: the son of the man who killed my mother and sister.

Jeramiah Abrum: the son of the man who started it all.

Gunfire comes next, and then from my place on the ground, the bottom part of my right leg is resting before my eyes. Only it isn't resting. Not really. It's seeping. It's bleeding. Pumping away and oblivious to the orphaned piece of meat it had become.

"Is he dead? IS RIDER DEAD?" I wasn't. Not as Mapone hoped. One well-placed bullet later and a man I should have put down myself is finally no more. His ticket punched, he falls awkwardly, the remaining part of his skull hitting the edge of the desk as gravity continues to do what it has always done best.

Next is haze. Followed by an introduction I come to understand seconds before Jeramiah tells me who he is—coming as he tourniquets my leg in an attempt to staunch the flow. Then it's the back of a vehicle I'm in, and the moon sits behind me and to the left. Or was it the right? More blood comes. More pain. Then Batista. A hospital bed that wasn't a hospital bed at all and finally, Jeramiah again. He's holding a prosthetic. Explaining everything as though it had just occurred. All of it jumbled. All of it jigsawed.

But it all comes rushing back as I look to the axe lodged in what had been passing as my foot for years. There's no blood this time. No pain. And because of this I'm afforded a few key seconds before Mancini clues in.

I take the moment.

And place the sawed-off to the side of the small man's stubbled cheek and watch as his unbelieving face is replaced by air. The bone shards this creates, mixed with a mist that wasn't really a mist at all, painting a pair of bookshelves full of DVDs in a way I've yet to tire of.

"Rider?" Jeramiah. Coming up behind me, his own piece out and at his side. In front of me now, looking down at the axe and the shot prosthetic it resided in, he takes the handle and tugs it free. "You want me to say I told you so now, or later?"

Man had a point. Didn't mean I was going to answer.

What I do say, however, is what I have said for longer than I can remember.

"Bring the axe."

"I have a bad feeling about this, Bishop." And granted, seeing how Mancini got the jump on me as he had, I should have listened. In the end, geography prevailed, and to the detriment of the prosthetic I most used, why I had decided to visit shitbird number one first instead of shitbird number two.

All told, Jeramiah won.

Which meant we had to hit the Ronson place on the way to finishing what we set out to do. The smallest of the three safehouses we used, it stood closest to the heart of Culver, the soundproofed basement and machinery it housed currently empty. But as with life, things have a way of changing on a dime.

"That the original model?" It was. Not as sleek as what I'd been using, but the balance it provided is all I was concerned about. Swapped out and locked into place, we turn back to the task at hand. Holdovers of a subscriber list created by a man who'd been in the ground for years.

Kincaid.

Mancini and the soon-to-be-greeted Burke remnants of a pedophile ring that never should have been. Brashness allowed this to occur—back to a time I felt leaving a message might work better that simply separating limbs. I learned, however. And adjusted my ways.

But men like Mancini and Burke, men who would suggest time caused people to forget, they continued to pop up every now and then, even decades after the fact. Sometimes it led us places, connecting and enlightening us to other things, depraved things, but more times than not the opposite occurred and we would find ourselves where we never wanted to be: the end of the line. With Burke, I hoped it would be the former. But if it wasn't, it didn't matter. One less shitbird was one less shitbird.

My favorite type of odds.

Where Mancini had been thin and bird-faced, Curtis Burke was bald and deep into the physical side of life. Wide across the chest and shoulders, he opens the door in boxers, flip-flops, and a Bud Light Lime in his hand. But there is no greeting from this man, nor do I offer one of my own. It's only our eyes and how they instantly narrow to slits. To his credit, he backpedals in an attempt to stand his ground, but by then it's too late.

Aged or not, I'd never not been fast.

Jeramiah closes the door behind us, goes about collecting Burke's phone and computer while I bind the man in front of a scuffed but sturdy-looking apothecary table.

"Change of plans," I say when Jeramiah returns. He says nothing. Only smiles. Then heads for the van.

Positioned to the right of the stairs and down another couple of steps, the apothecary table stood centered and surrounded by custom leather chairs and a dark red sofa. Behind this couch sat music equipment—guitars and whatnot, mic stands, a keyboard, and further down in a corner, a set of drums. Not a studio by any stretch of the imagination, no, but trying to be one all the same— the walls adorned and plastered with laminated vinyl by artists who never saw their thirties. The apothecary table is thick, made from solid oak, but it's only part of the reason I decided against taking Burke back to the safehouse. If I'm honest, I can be selfish. We all can. And if I continue laying down the truth, it goes back to Mapone. To what his man had taken from me and how it had been done. It wasn't the be-all/end-all, as most scenarios ended up presenting themselves, but neither could I deny how prevalent a specific instrument had become in the way I went about things.

"I see you're awake. I know you're scared." Wrists and ankles bound to the legs of the table, he lay prone and straining, a ceiling fan above him and set on high. Gagged, he raises his head toward my voice, the cords of his neck like wire as he holds my gaze. It was an added touch, sure, but one born of necessity, as the table could only hold so much of his frame.

More to the point, I had big plans for the space between his thighs.

Jeramiah removed the gag.

"I have money. It's yours. All of it. Whatever you want. Anything!"

People like Burke, they will always be different. Thinking they can buy themselves out from whatever they're about to be crushed by. Most times it works. With me, it never would.

"It's not money I'm after, Curtis. You think hard enough, I'm sure a big boy like you can come to understand the reasons as to why." I wouldn't bet on it, though. Just priming the pump is all. Attempting to squeeze a name.

He relaxes, the back of his skull now down and hanging over the edge of the table. Jeramiah moves round, hunkers down. "Bishop here, he's being nice. Tell you what. You tell us everything you and Mancini had going on the side, we won't even mention Kincaid."

And just like that, it all falls apart. Denial after denial coupled with rage. Which, percentage-wise, was about half the time. Only when the tears begin do we usually find ourselves close to getting what we want.

Cue Mancini's axe and its first bite into the wood in front of Burke's boxered junk. It gets his attention. Vibration and sound first, of course, followed by saucer-like eyes as his head snaps back up.

"I think he's beginning to see it from our point of view, Bishop. What do you say, Curtis, a little off the top and we call things square?"

It nets us a name. But only one. Even after I dig into the meat of his right shoulder. Could there have been more? Possibly. But by then, the shock had taken hold, his bleeding too profuse, and exposed as it was, the underside of his neck had been speaking to me in ways too hard to ignore.

And I want to say I continued to be the man I used to be, that it only took one swing. But I can't, not as I'd like. It also means I venture back to where this began, to Mapone's office, as the big man sits behind his desk, the caverns of his eyes as empty as I remember them.

Is he dead? IS RIDER DEAD?

Not yet, Mapone. Not fucking yet.

LOW BONES

Rope thin, Bowman is smaller than the five-two he puts to paper. Doesn't stop his eyes from widening into doorknobs once he realizes it's his own left arm Jeramiah is holding.

"I want you to think hard about the hurt you've caused in your life, Larry. I want you to realize I'm attempting to distill it down for you."

Larry looks to his left, to the melted mound of scar tissue the shoulder there had become, then down the length of his body that lay vertical and strapped to a surgical table. We're in the basement of the Buchannan house, in what I'd come to call the White Room. Behind us, jutting up like a metal neck and calling, sat Ray's crowning achievement: an incinerator that ran through the foundation and escarpment beneath, releasing into the ravine at the back of the property.

"How…"

"Does it matter?" Jeramiah replies. "We know who you are. We know what you are. Larry, we found you." True story. Going back to a man who got the jump on me, a man by the name of Mancini. Coming at me with an axe from around a corner in his own basement, Mancini swings wildly, savagely, but this excessiveness does him no favors. The axe coming to rest within a part of me that no longer existed and hadn't for quite some time. The confusion this gives birth to—me unreactive to an axe going through what should very well consist of muscle, tendon, and bone—gave me what most would call the high ground and, in an instant, the sawed-off is off its leash, barking for all its worth. Hell, I may have even winked.

But it's not over, not by a mile. Sending us to where Jeramiah thought we should have gone in the first place: Curtis Burke. Mancini's partner in crime.

A full foot shorter by the time we're done with him, by the very same axe that took apart my prosthetic I might add, the name Burke gives up is Bowman, Larry G.

"And Larry, I want you to really see what I'm doing here. I want you to believe." Jeramiah continues to point at the man using the man's own arm. One move more and he takes the limb by each end and, joint down, slams it into his raising knee. The sound is instant, unmistakable, and as skin gives way to bone, the dead flesh ruptures. But the blood that comes is darker than what we're used to—both sluggish and thick. Larry releases a kind of moan-scream, and his head, strapped or not, strains and tries to jerk like a man who thinks he's dreaming and wishes to wake.

Perfection, in other words. In every possible way.

But Jeramiah, he isn't done. Moves forward and pushes the severed appendage up and into Bowman's protesting mouth, a shard of protruding bone spearing the man's cheek in the process.

"I want you to sing, Larry. I want you to think hard about every associate you've even had. I want you to say their names out loud. You do that, your head, it doesn't become your arm."

It doesn't take much after that. For truth, it rarely did. Not once we prove how far we're willing to go. Further still, and Bowman's introduction to the incinerator commences, but that, of course, had been a given from the start—him giving us what we hoped to get from him or not. In turn, it brought forth the night's final act—Bowman's variation of a plea I'd heard too many times to count. The *I'm sick*. The *I'm broken*. The *I promise to get help*.

Some accepted the fact better than others, sure, but the majority did not. Either way, it had become part of the process. And good, bad, or indifferent, I only cared that they knew they could not escape what they themselves had set in motion.

It's why they had to burn.

We tail Robillard for a month before we narrow it down to an abandoned, dilapidated farmhouse outside Hanson Falls. Jeramiah watched through binoculars from afar twice. The second time, of course, sealing the deal. And we didn't know for certain the name Bowman gave us would prove true, but yeah, Robillard's second visit to the house, a house his parents left him but he did not live in, sent up all the right kind of flags.

"Gym teacher does, in fact, have a hobby, Bishop. You're not going to like what it is, though." He was right, of course, but like most things we involved ourselves in, I'd seen my fair share. Every once in a while, however, some dirtbag chooses the unthinkable, deciding that this life and no other was the time to go above and beyond.

Enter Samson Robillard. All six foot, two inches of him. Round face and a rounder stomach, his marriage certificate said he'd been playing at being human for sixteen years. The same amount of time he'd been teaching physical education at the high school he'd graduated from.

But it wasn't the farmhouse I was going to be interested in, Jeramiah informs. Nor the roofless barn that sat crumbling to its right. No, it was what lay in the field beyond.

"He's been at this for years, Bishop. Decades even." When I see the well for myself, I can't disagree. The lower bones dry and brittle looking. The ones that made up the top of the pile, not so much. The opposite, in fact. It's the near pristine *Hello Kitty* t-shirt that my flashlight comes to rest upon that destroys me, however. It does more than destroy me, though. It enrages me.

It also ensured Robillard wouldn't just die.

It ensured he'd suffer.

* * *

The sun is out and it's mild, but my breath still plumes.

"Keep walking," I say, but when Robillard fails to pick up the pace, Jeramiah jabs the butt end of the sawed-off into the middle of the man's back hard enough to send him to the ground. Knees in the snow, he stays there, his head bowed, and then his body begins to hitch. He's wearing blue chinos, a blue windbreaker, and unlaced boots that had seen better days.

"Don't bother," I say, and Jeramiah reads me like a book, the metal now down and resting upon the back of Robillard's neck at an angle. Robillard stands and plods on—resumes what began that morning and would be finishing soon.

And the man had no idea, not until he turned the corner from the barn, making his way back to his Caprice.

"Help you?" To his credit, he sounded normal enough. He wasn't, though. All told, they never are.

"That depends," I say, and Jeramiah raises the gun, "on what your definition of that word entails."

Did he know at this point in time? Possibly. I choose to believe he put it together as we walked. Either way, he turns on his own when we finally reach the well. Snow surrounds it. Not as much as the day Jeramiah showed me what it contained but enough to see the oil we'd left behind.

"Name them," I say, and the man just stands there, nose and eyes leaking, a combination of fear and bewilderment fighting for dominance upon his face.

"*Name. Them.*" He does. Of course, he does. And he could have missed one, but no, I don't think he did—the corpses beneath us like trophies to men like Sam Robillard. Trophies he could no longer touch but felt compelled to visit all the same.

It was enough. More than.

And same as the anonymous phone call I knew we'd eventually make, I push him over the edge.

He screams the entire way down, all twenty feet or so, and

howls once he reunites with solid ground—with the prepubescent bodies that break his fall. I peer over the edge, the tips of my gloves pressing into the motor oil we'd used to coat the inner stone. No child could have climbed their way out of there, if in fact they'd been alive once they found themselves trapped within, but a full-grown adult was a different story entirely.

Did it change anything? Would it?

Then as well as now, I have to believe it did.

But something remained, and it pulled at me.

Begging the question: was it possible for a husband to adequately hide sixteen years of depravity from someone they lived with? The possibility existed, sure, but the percentage it required, this is what I couldn't back away from—rising in my mind like the image of the well itself, old and made of stone. The skulls come to me next, discarded like trash and far from fully grown. Most are fleshless. Others decompose. The angles of the lower bones suggesting it hadn't been pain they felt at the end, but agony.

And the wife, she kept coming back to me. How broken down, they say marriage is but two lives becoming one.

"I'll be honest, Bishop. The thought, it crossed my mind." We were alike, Jeramiah and 1, but it hadn't always been this way, not from the start. When he tells me he'd already set up a feed, however, I realize just how in line our thinking had become.

Time to finish the work.

It takes two days. Her blue Toyota parking in front of the farmhouse as feed one catches her arrival. It's night, past eleven, with camera feed two picking her up behind the barn as she makes her way toward the well. Flashlight swaying back and forth, she's a bigger woman, husky, wearing a wool hat and dressed for winter in ways her husband hadn't been.

She plods on. Her girth a hindrance through the slush. But she doesn't stop, not until she reaches her destination. I watch as she brings the flashlight up and peers over the edge. I watch as her head moves up and down. It let me know two things at once: that a little bit of Samson Robillard still remained, and what I wanted to occur, it continued to happen as planned.

What it also let me know was what a part of me had known from the start, male, female, or otherwise.

It means we walk in on Monica Robillard mid pack, and if I'd taken Jeramiah up on his hypothetical, one that bet against Monica Robillard returning to that well by her own volition, I'd have been wrong.

"No rope?" Jeramiah asks, and uses the cattle prod to point to the suitcase. It worked both ways, sure, but more importantly put an end to the discussion we'd started as we followed her home in the van.

Monica screams, shimmies sideways, and grabs her ample chest. Her hair is fire red, long, and matted from her hat.

"What...who are you?"

We're in her bedroom, the blue Samsonite she'd placed upon the unmade bed already half full. When neither of us answer, it's almost as if you can see her putting it together.

"He made me...I never knew...not at the start." Her hands roll into one another, thumb pocket massaging thumb pocket, and when we fail to respond a second time, she tries a different approach and offers her mouth while going to her knees. It's not the first time something like this had occurred. From experience, it probably wouldn't be the last.

Uninterested, Jeramiah moves forward and extends the cattle prod. The woman spasms, gurgles, and then falls to the side. When she begins to come around, we're already halfway between the well and the barn, her arms trailing behind her and leaving tracks in the snow. She moans, moans again, and then the leg I have hold of becomes a live wire bucking for release.

Jeramiah drops his leg and re-ups the cattle prod, the underside of a second, smaller chin his new area of interest.

We reach the well.

As I did not do seventy-two hours prior, I take my flashlight and peer over the edge and find the man. He looks different today, less robust. Makes me think he might actually learn something before he leaves this world.

"I want you to know she threw you under the bus, Hoss. Most people see you in the position you've found yourself in, they tend to want to help. When they decide to run, well, that's the shit that speaks loudest of all."

He looks up to me then, and I notice his face—how the skin on *his* skull still remained. How the bones of *his* arms were still covered in flesh. Had he been eating the snow that came to him? I didn't know, but the betting part of me said I'd probably make money if I let things ride.

"Anyway, I thought you'd want to know is all. Give you a little something to discuss in the dark perhaps." His eyes go a little bit wider at that, and as Jeramiah yells, *"Incoming,"* we hoist Monica Robillard up and over the edge. She doesn't land on her husband as you might think, and she's still out cold as we drop her, but we hear parts of her break regardless.

Did it change things? Would it?

Again, I have to believe it did.

NEW WAR, SAME AS THE OLD WAR

Same as the time I tied Alex's large intestine to the trailer hitch of a now disappeared van, and same as the time I left a limbless and unconscious Kincaid in that wheelchair as the meth house burned behind him, I had to slow things down after what we found in the well. Not only because of Jeramiah's anonymous phone call but because of the speculation and subsequent media explosion it caused once the number of bodies had been totalled.

Back to the front page, in other words, and the shadows I have tried my hardest to keep to in jeopardy of being erased.

Alex had been a mistake made in the heat of the moment, and one a great many camera phones caught at the time. Fortunate, every angle out there captured the van from behind, recording not who'd been behind the wheel but every scream Alex let loose that day and every piece of his insides that learned how to fly.

Kincaid, however, is the mistake I continue to atone for, and if given the chance, remained one of two things I'd change if I could.

Letting Kincaid live allowed him to create a network larger than the one I thought I'd ended. I was wrong, of course, but leaving him outside that meth house, attempting to use the image as a message, it too attracted unwanted attention, and again I'm forced to slow things down.

But Samson and Monica Robillard, how they're found at the bottom of that well, it tips my hand, and certain individuals begin to put stock into what most believe to be bumps in the night.

Editorial pieces, thy name is months.

And sure, focus is placed upon the other bodies pulled from that well, and closure is achieved for some. But for longer than I wanted, the spotlight failed to recede.

As with all things, though, the lights around the Robillard case finally do subside, and in time we're able to put things back into drive. However, it's what Jeramiah discovers while we're dark that sets the agenda. Showing me what I have at times forgotten: that mistakes aren't just meant to define us.

They're meant to set us free.

A different man, a younger man, would argue this claim in ways I can still remember. I've seen too much, however. Removed too many. And even though I ascribe and strive for a better world, the patience this requires remains a pill I fight hard to swallow.

"His phone was clean, Bishop. But his laptop held a name I think you're going to want to see." Curtis Burke was the name of the man the laptop belonged to. Headless now, he'd been a link in a very predictable chain, one that connected pieces of shit to pieces of shit and then for variety, other pieces of shit.

Once we'd disposed of him, Jeramiah gets to work on his electronics, the ones we left his residence with.

But Bowman came first, then the name *he* spits forward: Robillard.

Which meant it's almost a year to the day that I come to understand a certain strain of shitbird decided to set up shop in Culver once more. Holdovers I missed the first time around or something brand-new, I didn't know. But because of the money Jeramiah followed and how it led to a very specific picture of a very specific yacht, I was about to find out.

The Rabbit Hole is the name of the yacht in the picture Jeramiah comes across. Burke is on the bow, as built and as bald as the day I remove his head, and sandwiched between a handful of Armenians that end up becoming fish food back before the Towers fell.

"O'Bannon was in play here, right?" He was. A dirty cop if there ever was, Sid O'Bannon escapes me at the end, a sort of "the one who got away," but not before he points me in the direction I needed to be. One that connected me to a house full of infants being filmed in ways that breaks me still.

Children removed, I unpack a bone saw and go to work on appendages opposite to the ways I had in Kuwait. I make a recording of the festivities as well, meant to be viewed as a warning, but even this O'Bannon had gotten a hold of and altered.

And now here we were, years later, a money trail and an old picture pulled from a dead man's laptop, grinning at me from the past.

"Every file has been gone through twice and cleaned. There's nothing about O'Bannon." We're at Buchannan, and Jeramiah is seated and pointing to the screen. He stops, swivels in his chair, and then stands. "But Burke protected nothing, Bishop. *Nothing.* Their names and addresses, they're all there. We play this right, it's like a goddamn fucking do-over. We do this right, we make them see."

Mistakes, as I said, they can sometimes set you free.

Not totally, as I'll never forgive myself for Kincaid, but these Armenians, I always wondered if I'd gotten them all that night on the pier. The strong bet was no, but retaliation never came, and all roads that first led me to them dried up in the end. Until now, anyway.

But still, we kept it slow, and once we agreed on what had to be done, we come to realize we'd need to bring in a few of Jeramiah's guys to pull it off. All told, it's the only way timed abductions can work.

Most of them are heavyset and drowning in manicured facial

hair. Not Jeramiah's guys, but the Armenians we target. Their number in the warehouse totalling six by the time we have them strung up by the wrists. Weeping openly, this thinnest one wets himself once he sees Jeramiah and the clown mask.

I move to the tripod. Hit the On button and begin to record.

"I probably killed some of your fathers," I say, failing to give the camera my face. In a different setting, under similar circumstances, this would not be the case, but those days belong to a younger man, a stronger man. A man who eventually understands mistakes not for what they are but for what they can, in fact, become. "I probably put down some of your brothers, too. Seeing as I remember a few female screams, the possibility exists I made fish food of a mother or sister as well." A thick mole above a ruined right eye, the fourth one from the left begins to buck when I mention this, his body twisting and bumping into its neighbors as he screams at me from behind the gag. Jeramiah walks back into frame, takes the man hard by the chin, squeezes, and in under twenty seconds we're back to the task at hand.

"I'm going to read between the lines here. I'm going to go ahead and say I've struck a nerve. Stories, though, they have more than one side. I'm here to make sure you understand why."

I go on, but the men in front of me are not my target audience. They hear it, true, but my words and the recording are not meant for them. They were for each and every contact found on Burke's computer.

The message would be clear.

The message would be concise.

And as Jeramiah brings the chainsaw to life and it eats through flesh until innards sway and vertebrae drop, I continue to think of things I've done and things I'd yet to. How mistakes have allowed me to live to fight another day and how men like the ones now dangling in front of me would still be in the world if I had chosen anything other than what I had.

If anything, I concentrate on that.

* * *

It's an abattoir by the time we're finished—an ever-expanding lake of internal organs, human excrement, and legs that end in flip-flops and the type of footwear certain men use to make themselves look taller than they were.

I pan down, zoom in, and then zoom back out once Jeramiah returns with the end of our message. The yellow apron and clown mask still slick and dripping, he stands in front of what remained of Mole man and releases the cards from his chest. Sign one read FOLLOW THE CHILDREN. Sign two: WE'RE COMING FOR YOU. Sign three, PREPARE, was really just an extension of sign two, but I linger on it as it hits the ground and watch as it's overtaken by blood.

Sign four? Sign four was yet to be. Meaning men would either run from this or we'd continue. They'd accept what they deserved or rail against it.

Either way, a new war had just begun.

THE SECRET HISTORY OF BISHOP RIDER

It's not every day you wake up to find yourself gagged and hanging from chains in a warehouse now, is it? Nor find that the man in front of you, the man entrusted with your care I might add, he just *won't* shut the fuck up either. Yeah, not every day, agreed.

But Tabatha, for real, if you tried a fraction harder, enough to see your actions for what they are, I guarantee we'd get to the bottom of things a whole lot quicker. No, really, I kid you not. But since it's clear you're adamant in resisting this narrative, it allows me to understand two things at once. One, your personality type will never accept any type of responsibility for your actions, and two, it may be time for some context.

What? You don't care for context either? Tabatha. Tabatha, Tabatha, Tabatha. Not many of your kind do.

So, the secret history of Bishop Rider. Nah, I kid. Well, sorta. I mean, you don't know the *whole* story. The parts that bring us together today are what I'm talking about. You have the bones as to how certain things came to be, sure—most lowlifes do. The sister, the mother, the men in masks. But it's more than that. More than their murders, more than the gang rape, and certainly more than that video that's circulated. Only way for you to know such things is if you were, oh I don't know, part of a team, say. But even then, those chains you're in, ours *and* yours, they'd hold you back.

Yes, indeed.

Because it's never been about saving people, Tabatha. No, it's about stopping them.

I can't take credit for those words either. Nope, they come straight from the big man himself. But I get it. I do. Better yet, I understand.

He's attempting to stop people like you at the source, Tabatha. Kudos to him for attempting this too. I mean, I'm not privy to all of it, but the stuff I do see? Fuck me.

Bottom feeders, the goddamn fucking lot of you.

But like I said, there's a team. A group of like-minded individuals, you might say. A man by the name of Ray, he installed those very chains you hang from. Friends from a war from before my time, Ray has over the years built other things for Rider. Things that may or may not go bump in the night.

Anyway…

Back home from said war, Bishop, he finds he's no longer the man he once was and his time as a cop, it becomes a thing of the past as well. Having your mother found facedown in dumpster water will do that. Oh yes. Indeed. And this, Tabatha, is even before I mention that Rider's sister has yet to be found. Takes about four years for this to shake loose, and even then, there's no body, Tabatha, just that tape. That video of six men in masks.

You understand the importance of what I'm saying here? If so, it'll make what's coming somewhat easier to digest. If not, well, I'd like to think I'll care, but no, I don't think I will.

Now, where was I? Oh yes. But Rider's old partner, a detective named Batista, he's sympathetic to Rider's plight…to that video, and well, you could say an alliance was born. I'm not going to sugarcoat it either, Tabatha. These actions we take, it's because of people like you. In *response* to people like you.

Brings us to Chris DiLeo, Tabatha. And yes, there it is. Bill, tell her what she's won! I kid, of course, but yeah, panic is a truly unruly bird, isn't it? Brings baggage is what it does. Fight or flight and not much in between. It means DiLeo gave you up, Tabatha, and he did so before even one of his body parts was removed. Said it was all you, every idea. You who lured the girls, you who pimped them out. He was just the muscle, there to keep them in line. That true, Tabatha? Not that it matters much, not now, but you being you, a woman I mean, and preying upon those girls as you did. It takes it to another level if I'm honest. A monster's monster, as it were. But it goes beyond that, doesn't it?

Tabatha. Tabatha, Tabatha, Tabatha. We know it all, as I've said. Every last detail regarding who and what you are. Hell, I know what fucking flavor of Pop Tart you had for breakfast this morning.

That fire, Tabatha, it didn't start itself. And those four girls they found locked in that closet, they didn't place themselves there. Not with that deadbolt engaged from the outside as it was. You are truly a different kind of breed. You are truly…

Well, would you look at that: seems our time together is coming to an end. The big dude in black back there, that'd be Rider. The bigger one with the beard: Batista. And those jerry cans they're bringing our way? Unleaded, Tabatha. And no, they won't be needing all their contents. Not once the flames take hold. But what I think you should be concentrating on isn't the gasoline, Tabatha, but what's going to occur before they turn you to ash. They are going to make it last, Tabatha. They are going to ensure you bleed. It means you are about to have the day you deserve. It also means your time upon this earth is just about done.

Last thing, sweetheart. Tell DiLeo we say hi.

BIG TOOL PRODUCTIONS

It's been said there are multiple versions of the person we think we are. Variations of the reflection, some might say. There is the past self, the future self, and how we are perceived by others, just to name a few. Some of these variations are trauma-based, defining those who've been touched in ways many will never understand. Others are fortunate enough to sidestep such land mines. Others still, they excel at absorbing said trauma and using it not only to the best of their ability, but in ways they feel they must.

Me, I'm this last one. Unwanted, embraced, or otherwise.

"You have two hours max," Batista says, and the detective's voice, it held an edge I'd heard before. "I can't push the follow-up any longer. And Rider..." he stops here, and that edge, I can tell it's pregnant. "Do what you have to. Do what I know you're going to. From the looks of what they've done to her, the world will be better off with these fuckers off of it." True. All of it. But I knew that even before I picked up the phone. Batista needed to hear himself say it is all, and I couldn't blame him. Killing coming as easy to me as it came hard to him. He'd come around, sure, and by the time our partnership ends, he ends up being more like me than he'd probably care to admit.

Not that it mattered all that much, and Batista, I'm pretty sure he knew this already, but premeditated murder, for all the closure it can bring, it wasn't the only thing that drove me. I could pinch hit, in other words. And opportunity, when presented, was something I rarely turned down.

Not if I could help it.

He looks at me like I'm an insect. To him, I probably was. It gets the door open to the penthouse suite anyway, and then I'm all the way in the room. Incense berates me, potent, followed by hard liquor, stale popcorn, and staler sweat.

Sizing them up, only one of the three looks like trouble. Looks have a way of being deceiving, however, and as many a dirtbag can no longer attest, I am living, breathing proof of this fact.

"They told me this suite was soundproof," Goldilocks says, his goatee up and jutting as he speaks "I don't understand how a noise complaint…" I hold up one gloved hand. "I'm not here to pretend. Those cameras, those tripods, that girl who escaped and is right now in a hospital room giving her statement, that's why I'm here." I watch the bald one at the table freeze. I see the one in glasses on the couch turn toward him. Goldilocks, though, he's unencumbered by my words and on me as I thought he might be. The wax-on/wax-off scenario he presents, however, I did not see coming.

He lets loose a roar too but overextends as he comes into me, and in under four seconds I dip, grab, and pull his arm down onto my shoulder until I hear bone erupt from his skin.

My boot is next—the pig knife hidden within. I look to Baldy and Glasses, each like the wildlife I pegged them for.

I kneel down hard on Goldilocks's back, dead center between his shoulder blades. He exhales harder than he grunts, attempts to speak again, but I slide the knife into his right temple before he can utter a word. Glasses on the couch gasps, but Baldy, he stands, his chair hitting the carpet as he does.

"Now that I really have your attention," I say and use the back of Goldilocks's red button-down to wipe down the knife. I don't replace it back into my boot, though. No, there may still be use for it yet.

"You...you killed him. You killed Todd." Man had me there. Did I tell him he'd be next? If he didn't join Sunshine and me at the table? Yeah, I'm pretty sure I did.

"You're going to tell me who you're working for. I want distributors. I want who funds you. I want the people who supply you with the girls. You give me these things, you walk. You don't, I guarantee you end up worse than Todd here."

It's enough, and I see that each of them understands. What *I* didn't understand, however, is what I'd actually walked into; that in the span of the coming conversation, I'd be locked onto the white whale I'd been chasing for years.

"Chris DiLeo. Tabatha something," the bald one, Bruno, blurts out. "She's new. But she gets the girls. Chris brings them in. He calls, we come. I've never fucked them. I just record."

"You just record."

"Yeah, yeah. I never tou—" Too late, he realizes his mistake, and I'm on him before he can finish. The blade up through his left eye just as fast as my arm can manage. Glasses freaks out from my right and falls back as I follow Bruno down to the carpet. Both hands now, I push the knife as deep as physics allows. He twitches once, then nothing, and I feel him die.

"Anything, man. I'll do anything you want." The curtains are drawn but he's against them and shaking. "There's this other guy. Richie. His name is Richie. Easy money, he said. These girls, they come from Mexico. They have no prospects. Big Tool Productions is about providing prospects, he says. I'm sorry, man. I know it was wrong. I know. I was just doing a job. Please, I don't want to die."

But die he does. Not before names were repeated, though, and addresses were given, and I ensure he realizes who I was.

"You're...you're the brother?"

"I'm the brother."

If I'm honest, it's his eyes I remember most.

* * *

It happens fast after that. DiLeo the linchpin to Richie, and Richie the connection to the man behind a curtain I'd been trying to open for years: Marcel Abrum. Four years and countless bodies later: Abrum.

Geared up, I meet Batista at the usual spot. He's thinner now, and his face is drawn. Behind the lines, I see everything I need to—everything the both of us have sworn to correct.

"I've found him," I say and move forward, my eye line out toward Culver and down.

"Who?" And then it clicks; a pause as Batista goes and makes the leap. "Him? You're telling me Abrum is the guy?" I tell him more, plenty, how Marcel Abrum seemed to be the one who initiated it all.

Batista voices his concern, of course, cautioning that we could only take the information I received so far. I disagree and tell him as much, stating that this was it, there was no turning back—that after all this time, we had finally found the truth.

He takes a moment, a hand up and through what remained of his hair. He then jams his hands into the pockets of his overcoat.

Taking himself from the view of the lights below and the darkness beyond, he says, "What the fuck are we waiting for then?"

And if I recall, I don't answer. I didn't need to.

Abrum's strip joint comes next, us wearing the Kevlar before it. Helmets on, Batista takes the back, leaving me, and I see myself standing there in the dark, watching as it begins. Me entering. The nine of them in front of me.

I could deal with nine.

Abrum's death. His wife in pieces upon that stage and the parts of her overflowing from that wheelbarrow. The shotgun blast I take to the chest. Batista saving me. The thoughts that my time had run out.

But then I go further, deeper, and I'm reminded of the variations I'm destined to become. My future self, same as my past self, the same monster I have chosen to be.

Kincaid steps forward, then Mapone.

We all have demons. I continue to chase mine.

Images of a life I have lived the only way I felt I could. My leg. Batista's face. Ray's death. And more. More upon more. Alex's betrayal. Jeramiah's save. The men in those masks.

All of it. Every bit.

Multiple versions of a man who would come to embrace his hate and live off his rage. They deserve more, of course. They always have. But for those who were taken from me, I did what I could and became what was required to do so. And right or wrong, for good or naught, it's a choice I have chosen to live with. Even after I realized it may have chosen me.

For my mother and sister, I burned as many as I could.

HOSED

The White Room has always lived up to its name.

Built, rebuilt, and upgraded throughout the years, it sits beyond a wall of plexiglass at the far end of the basement of the Buchannan house. Floor to ceiling, a ceramic-polyurethane tile layers the soundproofed walls, running the entire square footage and grading toward a drain at the center. Hydraulic push button compartments open to reveal surgical equipment, overnight tools, and three different types of bone saw. The right side of the room holds one of two operating tables: one stainless steel, the other the same ceramic-plastic fusion that Ray used to reinforce the walls. Both tables can be inverted, both can restrain, and both are third in line as to what I cherish most about the room.

Behind me sat number one, Ray's crowning achievement: the incinerator. Not quite toward the back of the room, it rose from the floor like a metal neck, hungry, sleek, and a marvel to behold.

However, it's what Ray gifts to me before he dies that I'd be using today.

"If anything, it'll help with certain types of cleanup," Ray says, and we walk toward his last creation. Seven feet high, three feet wide, it sat adjacent to the plexiglass and resembled a hot water heater, but one more oblong than round. Modified, an industrial-sized hose slithered up and out from behind, the remainder coiled and hung beside the room's original cleanup hose. This hose being red, however, as opposed to the smaller green one we'd used for years.

"It'll depend on the type of mood you're in, I suppose, but knowing you, I'm sure you'll find a way to make it work best." He wasn't wrong, but I didn't say that at that time, and Ray is removed from the board not long after, the following year consisting of me taking apart the man who killed him and not much else. Hightower down all four appendages and a tongue by the time he succumbs.

It meant I'd never deployed the acid Ray set up.

It also meant Arjeet Singh, inverted and strapped to the table as he was, would be the first in a long line of men to experience what it could do.

Death may have stopped Ray, but it didn't *stop* Ray.

His work, an extension of my work, lived on.

An acid attack, or acid throwing, holds the intent to disfigure, maim, torture, or kill. Perpetrators of these attacks throw corrosive liquids at their victims, usually aiming for their faces. It is a horrid practice, inhuman, and has become more prevalent with each passing year.

Arjeet Singh brings it with him when he and his family migrate here. He doesn't implement what he views as his God-given right until years later, however, and only after his family has acclimated to western life and he felt he'd lost control, been disrespected one too many times, or any other nonsense the man hoisted as a defence.

"And five years being all the time you served, Arjeet, this is why we're together as we are. Why I felt we needed to talk." He's soft in middle, balding, with dark spots upon his cheeks and a mustache swallowed up by the gag. Still in the white button-down and paisley tie I find him in, the insides of his tan pants are a much different story, and one that continued to darken the more he realized I meant to see things through.

"What you did to them, I know you feel you were justified,

Arjeet, but you weren't. What you are is the opposite of what a father should be. What you are is what people like your wife and daughters come to dread in life. You are a cancer, Arjeet, nothing more."

He shakes his head, but again, it's nothing new. Men like Arjeet blinded not only to how they conduct themselves but resolute in their belief they have done nothing wrong. It's a sickness, really, and one that cannot be cured.

Not without help.

I put on the suit. I turn on the exhaust fans.

"If I'm honest, I have to say this was meant to be. You being the first person I'll be attempting this on. But if you need a reason, know I have thought of your family often these last few months. Of their lives and now, how they've been made to live them. This is why it has to be this way, Arjeet. This is why we are here. Also, I've seen the pictures."

His eyes go wider at that, and then his face falls in on itself, same as his shoulders. Resignation? Sure, let's go with that.

I step forward, my suit noisy as I do. I put on my mask. It's flat-faced, MIRA level, and more black than camouflage green. I place the same type of mask upon Arjeet and then walk back and uncoil the hose.

I turn.

And Arjeet, devil that he was, tries one last time to speak to me through his eyes.

I do not accept the invitation. The time for invitations had passed.

I start with his right knee.

The acid is quick, eats early, and propelled as it was, becomes a type of laser. Separated but held in place by the strap, the leg remains upright, a smoking, sliding mess. I aim up and hit the strap, but as it drops to the tile and rolls, I realize I've become a party of one—Arjeet and shock now one and the same.

No matter. I push on. The leg smokes, it disintegrates, and I continue to lather it until I see bone. Then I take the other leg, and both arms after that. I finish with the man's face, keeping the stream focused until the mask is no more. Flesh parts and parts again, falling away in chunks, and I can't say for certain, but yes, I breach the skull and witness brain. Arjeet Singh's body, by the end, sliding free of the remaining straps and becoming not quite a puddle of sludge, not yet, but in time a thin-enough substance that works its way toward the drain and is never seen again.

What I don't say to Arjeet is something I maybe should have—that he should have killed his family instead of maiming them. He does that, they never let him out. He does that, he never runs into someone like me.

Seeing firsthand the damage he'd brought into this world, I believe his wife and daughters would agree.

FOLLOW THE CHILDREN

It isn't until Jeramiah separates Kinley's left hand at the wrist with a cleaver that we get to where we needed to be. Which, truthfully, happened more times than a person imposing such reductions would ever think it could. Still, there we were.

Jack Kinley proving to be not only a hardcase but also the last rung on a very particular ladder. One I wished to extend but from experience knew I couldn't count on. Not when dealing with men who dealt in the unthinkable.

We're in the newest of the three safehouses we used, the one by the airport, and back before I light the night and use it as a morgue. I take out quite a few shitbirds when the foundation detonates, sure, but it ends with Ray's death by the time it all plays out. Unfortunate as that was, the positive born of the loss, it would lead us to situations similar to this, with men like Kinley sitting in similar chairs and similarly running their mouths.

"It's a swap house. They're fuck houses. It always is. Christ, you cut off my hand. You cut off my fucking hand!" And as he pulls the stump free of the table it'd been pinned to, the blood arcs as it continues to jet. The hand? It just sits there, leaking and inert on the other side of the cleaver.

Jeramiah returns with a towel.

"Hold it tight, Kinley. Be a shame if I had to take the other one before we let you go." He's a thick man, and like Jeramiah, hit the gym. And his face, the one that had been keeping a stiff upper lip, it was blunted now, sallow even. But make no mistake:

contrary to what Jeramiah said, Kinley wouldn't be leaving. I knew this. Jeramiah knew this. Kinley knew this. But the game, drowning in self-denial or not, it would continue to play out.

Speaking of denial.

"Okay. Okay. It's the money. It always talks. Fuck, I think you already know this."

We did. Of course, we did.

But what I wanted to know was the one thing we hadn't figured out.

"Tell me where they keep the girls."

Hanson Falls, though not quite the size of Culver, held a darkness of its own. It's here, just inside the city limits, we find the double-wide. The trailer had been tweaked, was on bricks, and at best now stood as a cage. Last time Kinley had been there, the number had been eight, he said. Possibly ten.

I make the call. Batista responds and, jurisdiction-bound, makes his own calls.

The world becoming a slightly better place in the process.

But it wasn't over. Not how we thought.

We had Kirby, the man whose property the double-wide sat upon, and Bilks, a fat man in overalls who we find living in a small shack to the right of the trailer. But what they give up as Billy's pigs start in on their feet is the stuff of nightmares. Scenarios more hellish than most care to admit but continue to happen upon this world every day.

"I'll make sure it goes slow," Billy says and places his only hand on my shoulder. It didn't help, and Billy knew it wouldn't, but old soldiers and habits have always had more in common than death.

It meant we'd never not try.

Ever since Ray installed the incinerator in the basement of the

Buchannan house, the time Billy and I spent together had been greatly reduced. The incinerator not exactly replacing him but shielding us in a way his pigs could not.

This is not to say Billy was no longer a part of the things. Like he'd been when we first met in Kuwait, he'd become more reserve than active is all, called upon whenever I felt the situation needed him most.

Hence Kirby and Bilks.

Child traffickers who, by the state of the grasslands we trespass upon, knew a thing or two about livestock as well. How it lived and what an animal's teeth were capable of. Fitting, in other words, and why Billy was prepared when I show up in the van.

"Long time, Rider." He's a little older, sure, but it's still Billy who greets me. From his camo fatigues to his unkempt hair to a smile as nonexistent as most of his teeth.

I tell the man it's been too long, and he nods, cutting through my headlights as he goes to open the barn's double doors. I pull in, get out, and one arm or not, Billy is bent set on helping remove my payload from the van.

The men strung up, Billy's hand now down off my shoulder, I offer him what I always offered: that I'd be in touch soon. In no way knowing just how soon that would be, and the chain of events we set into motion would not only come to end with a man we'd both been to war with losing his head, but a nonstop replay of the event that to this day has yet to leave me.

Like April and my mother, I dream of Ray.

Navarro is the name Bilks gives up. And long before Billy's hogs are even halfway to his shins. His details listed him as thirty-seven, five-eight, but after holding the pictures Jeramiah takes, I conclude the man's height included his boots. A receding hairline and close-set eyes gave him an older-than-he-appeared vibe, but it wouldn't matter, not once we took him apart.

"It's more than just money, Bishop." Jeramiah shows me

what he means. The invitations he intercepts had gone out encrypted, and in this moment, as I read the screen, I flash back to something similar, involving an auction, too many men, and an airplane hanger I leave bloodier than I found it.

"Better yet, listen to this." He'd tagged Navarro's cell as well, and not surprisingly, the recording involved many of the things I thought it would. The raid on the double-wide. The girls taken into custody by Hanson PD. The disappearance of Kirby and Bilks. But near the end of the conversation, I'm given something I don't often hear.

"It feels like something else is going on here," Navarro says, and the guy he's talking to, a deeper voice than Navarro, replies, "How do you mean?"

"How do I mean? I mean, I've heard the stories. I'm saying I've grown attached to my arms and don't want them to end up in a dumpster somewhere."

"Christ, you believe that shit? Eli, you worry too much. Ronnie and Cade will turn up. They probably caught wind of what was coming up the driveway and bolted when they did. You think it's anything more than that, maybe it's time you see a shrink."

There was more, of course, but what interested me most was the sit-down Navarro mentions when he fails to buy in on Deep Voice's explanation.

"No more get-togethers until it happens. I'm serious. Not one more boy."

Deep Voice pauses, his lack of patience audible. "You do not want to fuck with the money, Eli. You fuck with the money, I guarantee it will attempt to fuck back."

But Navarro would have none of it, and his tone seemed up to the task. A few more back and forths and Deep Voice relents, setting a time and place.

Jeramiah stops the recording.

I stand. He looks at me. I, him. "Make the calls," I say.

It was time to end this thing.

* * *

It's night, and Ray pulls his van up alongside ours. He has his ball cap on, the grey he never used to have now like wings above his ears. The big man sits in the passenger seat beside Ray, his windbreaker unzipped, his beard covering his scars as best it could.

Batista rolls down the window. "All good?" It was. Or would be soon. Two blocks over and an hour from this point in time to be precise.

"I want Navarro alive," I say, and Jeramiah nods as I look past him. "If it can happen. If it doesn't, we'll find another way."

They nod. I nod back.

We exit the vans.

"When I heard you mention this meeting place, I thought you might be kidding. But no, Navarro, it appears you are this cliché." He's still in shock, Deep Voice and the dead man in the passenger seat beside him still leaking from the parts of their faces Batista and Jeramiah left them with.

The top level of a parking garage we occupied overlooked strip clubs, fast food chains, and the largest of Culver's three casinos.

For men like Eli Navarro, it was probably the only way it could be.

From the left, up on the driver's side, came Batista. Jeramiah taking the right. Once Deep Voice rolls down his window and tells Batista to *beat it, jag-off, go hassle someone else,* he and Jeramiah unload two shots each, suppressed but far from noiseless.

I slide in beside Navarro in the backseat.

Again, shock held him, but the smell coming from the front seat was slowly being joined by a new one in back.

"Let's pull it together, Hoss. We have things to discuss," I say and twice snap my fingers beside his ear. It brings him round, but before I inject him with the syringe, I tell him what I'd been planning since hearing his voice on that tape. "You remember asking about dumpsters recently? Yeah, I thought you might. How around this city people sometimes find arms inside them?" He turns his head then, and it may have been miniscule, but yeah, the tremble was there.

"Surprise."

Ray pulls up two minutes later and keeps the van running as we do the transfer. Navarro's bound at the mouth now, same as his wrists, but the work was far from done. Names still needed to be named, arms still needed to be removed, and I hadn't forgotten about the boys he mentioned, the ones he'd threatened to withhold. We would get to them too. We would find them. And because I have already lived this part, I know we do—locating six more before Navarro exits the world and Batista decides it was time to pack it in.

Did his departure change things? Sure. But I don't blame the man.

All told, I never could.

Deep Voice's real name ends up being Mick Snow. The "money" in the passenger seat beside the late Mick Snow, Don Torres. Both prove ancillary in the end, and the only good they provide is what Jeramiah pulls from their phones.

"It cross-checks with Navarro. Grimes has to be the fourth man." He was, of course, but Grimes's name appearing in each of their contacts as it had, I didn't need it to be verified to know what it meant. In a different world, sure, but this was not a different world. This was anarchy hidden in the dark. And an evil that grew bolder every day. But we had another name now, and an address, and once we dig in and begin the re-con, the operation we'd uncovered comes into view.

It's unassuming too, the house, or innocuous. A bricked two-story ranch in the center of an average street in an average suburb of Culver. Jeffery Grimes himself was just as unassuming, in beige khakis, a Notre Dame pullover, and thick glasses that he wore upon an angular face.

"Help you?" he says as we walk up the drive. Jeramiah smiles, says, "Act natural," and then opens his jacket to show Grimes his Glock. "Just pretend we're old friends. Now put down the hose, make it look like you've invited us inside."

Inside, I waste no time and have Grimes against the wall and his hands zip-tied in under half a minute. He doesn't speak. He doesn't protest. And it's happened like this before, sure, but the instances that it had I can count on one hand.

"Move." He does. The three of us downstairs now, the hallway here filled with sports memorabilia, jerseys behind glass and the like. We press on, Jeramiah in front, Grimes in the middle, and me coming last. His shoulders are fully slumped now, further than when we first arrived, but same as what we were about to see, there was a reason this had occurred.

The room is filled with what I knew it would be. Monitors sitting to the left of us, banks of them, some screens being empty, others showing things no person should ever witness.

"I waive my rights. I admit to everything. I believe I deserve to be in jail." It catches me off guard. I freely admit this. But Jeramiah and his own rage is a step ahead of mine, and in a heartbeat he's on the man, tackling him to the ground, the butt of his gun out and into bone by the fourth swing. By the tenth, you'd be hard-pressed to say what was left could even be considered a face.

But Jeramiah, he continued to dig. Blood spatter and shards of bone like slick candy on the carpet by the time he gets off the man.

"I'd like to say you got him, but something tells me you already know that." A comedian I was not, but it pulls a smile from Jeramiah anyway. Either way, it ensures Jeramiah is wearing two sets of clothes by the time we finish what we'd set out to do.

We copy it all.

In the end, we come to understand that Navarro and Grimes recorded everything. The total number of clients equalling six hundred and twelve. Cross-referenced against payment type and we come up with two hundred and twenty actual names. Could we get them all? No. Not how I wanted. But we could adapt, and we do, in time exposing each of them to not only their spouses, but their mothers, their fathers, and any other family member Jeramiah could connect them to. And four days later, after a conversation involving a "blood could in fact run thicker than water" type of scenario, Jeramiah goes one better and in the subject line types FOLLOW THE CHILDREN before he embeds each email with the video link they starred in and sends it to Culver PD via the IP address from Grimes's home computer.

Was it a mistake? Maybe. And only because it put us on a different type of radar. But here now, looking back, I can say if given the chance, I'd do it the same way again.

I like to believe most of us would.

BIRDS OF A FEATHER

"I'll be honest, Keeko, I thought I was done with you." More to the point, I thought I'd already killed the man.

But no, there he was, one of the faces Jeramiah couldn't attach a name to with regards to the Navarro/Grimes house and the recordings we find there. Of the six hundred separate individuals we *do* find, Jeramiah could only match two hundred or so. But lo and behold, paired with fresh eyes and an extremely effective double-check, a man I'd fed the exterior wall of a nightclub to stares back at me with eyes two decades older than the last time I'd looked into them.

"But people like you have an ability to survive when you shouldn't. I also admit to not knowing you had something like this within you." He strains against his binds, the lean muscle of his small frame rolling like leather. His wrists behind him and ankles bound to the legs of the chair, we're in the man's own kitchen, the fridge humming to our left, and sweat runs from us both. Some borne of exertion. More borne of fear.

"I mean, I find out after the fact that Alex was into Mapone as he was, but being into kids, that wasn't Alex. But finding you on that recording as we did, it made me think of other things. More specific, other people. Three guesses as to who." I hoped I was wrong, because if I wasn't, it meant years ago I'd had two in my grasp and allowed them both to walk. Granted, I didn't think Keeko would survive his sudden diet of brick, but Meat Sleeves, him I'd presented a choice, and smart man that he was, he answers correctly, giving up Alex in the process.

That was the end of it—their part, anyway.

Alex's demise was different, of course, consisting of betrayal, skin being scraped from bone, and more of his insides on the outside by the time he detaches from the van. But now, almost twenty years removed, Keeko Reyes in a chair, the left side of his jaw still crooked from our first encounter, I lower his gag and ask him to consider carefully the words he was about to say.

"Fuck you, Rider." I understood. It was all he felt he had. All most of them feel they have by the time we get to here. When the hammer comes up, though, and I dig into where I'd left off, it becomes what it always became—what some of them tend to forget. This was an end as well as a means to an end.

He would answer my questions either way.

The study held a desk, soft light, and bookshelves from floor to ceiling on either side. A small couch ran to the right of me, from my position in the doorway, and it's from here I watch as Jerry "Meat Sleeves" Talon first notices my reflection in the window in front of his desk. He tenses, his hand instinctively shooting out toward the top drawer on the right side of the desk.

"Don't bother," I say, and the man, a man who once ripped the forearm skin of another man clean off and received a nickname because of it, pauses there, then retracts his hand and lowers his head while simultaneously swivelling his chair to face me.

He's not as bulky as I remembered him, but his bull nose remained intact. The loops in his ears no longer hung as they had either, leading me to believe he'd had surgery to correct what he'd done to himself when he'd been young. In a Ramones V-neck, crocs, and blue track pants, he seemed like half the bouncer I once put a hammer through.

"I've dreaded this day for longer than I can remember. Even after you said you'd never bother me again. I want you to know that." Good memory. I didn't have clue one as to what he was on about, however.

"I don't let many men live," I say. "Not once I find out."

"I never fucked no one who didn't want it. And I never fucked no kids." He says these words proudly, vehemently—like it might change what I already knew.

"I never said you did."

He nods. "But yet here you are."

"Here I am."

"I have a wife now, you know. She's due back soon."

Now it was my turn to nod. "Beverly, I know. But Jerry, let's not go there. A man like me doesn't do what he does for as long as I have without being thorough." It meant she left for "bridge night" a half hour ago, leaving Jerry and me with all the time we'd require.

"Please," he says, and I see the water well in his eyes, then flow. "I told you, I never fucked no kids."

"I believe you, Jerry. But it's not the reason I'm here."

"Then why?"

"I think you know."

"I don't. I don't. Rider, seriously, I don't." But I give him nothing. I only stand there in the doorway, the hand in my coat pocket still pretending to hold the gun that wasn't there.

"Because I knew? You're here because you think I knew?" He was getting warmer, but more specifically, he *did* know. On top, he chose to do nothing with the information as he could have.

"It's not because I think, Jerry." And then I move forward, my hand out from my pocket and into my inside one. "It's because I know." And Jerry's eyes don't just open wide when he sees the hammer in my hand, they bug outward. PTSD? As I see a hand slide up under his jaw, I'd have to go with yes.

He pushes back into his chair, the chair now up against the desk. He tries to ward me off, tries to stand, but by the second strike he goes limp, and his hands fall, one into his lap and the other to his side. I hit him again. And again. Five times, six, and until I not only lose count but parts of his face start coming away in hunks. His body leaning to the left, blood descending to the carpet in strings, I reposition and hook the claw end of the hammer into the exposed side of his jaw. I have to use a foot for leverage, but the mandible gives way in time, and I drop what comes at his feet, the flesh still attached more ragged than whole.

I picture Alex. I picture Reyes. How they and what remained of Jerry connected to me in ways that anger me still. It brings up Mapone, my leg, and every piece of shit we'd put down since. I think of yesterday. I envision tomorrow. Active participants and silent ones. It didn't matter. They were all game, peripheral or otherwise. Where there was one, there would always be another. We would seek them out regardless. We would show each of them the error of their ways.

We would make them burn.

ADDENDUM

"Act, and the universe responds, Eli. Act, and the universe responds." His eyes alternate between squeezing shut and full-on doorknobs. I stand to the right of him, the incinerator over my left shoulder and deep into the room. Gagged, he's vertical and strapped to the table, but we still aren't eye to eye.

I move forward. Eli flinches, tries to shake his head and, controlled or not, does his best to become one with the stainless steel he's tethered to.

"Men like you fail to understand this. More to the point, you only heed the beginning part." True. And I'd seen it too many times to believe otherwise. Eli Navarro here being the living, and for the time being, breathing proof.

I learn of his existence by way of a man named Bilks who, by way of one-armed Billy, sells out Eli as the tendons in his feet begin taking up residence in the belly of Bill's pigs. Not the easiest way to go out, no, but certainly one of the loudest. It leads to Navarro, however, who in turn nets us a couple more dirtbags and, ultimately, Jeffrey Grimes, Navarro's partner in crime. Hiding in plain sight, Grimes is pure white picket fence when we enter his world, out front watering his grass and oblivious to the rage he was about to unleash.

"But even that's not entirely true, is it?" Eli continues to push back against the table, and by the smell, he'd worked up enough liquid to darken his pants yet again. "And the thing about selfishness, Eli? It can only take a man so far." I bring up the hatchet then, turn it once, and as he himself thought I would, proceed to dig into the meat of his right shoulder until I hit bone. His nightmare coming true, I share the wealth and move on to his other arm, but it's too much for old Eli and he bleeds out before it drops to the tile. Same as the rest of him, it makes its way into the incinerator, and then in no short order it was onto Grimes, his lawn watering, and how Jeramiah relieves the man of his face.

Not to say such a reduction wouldn't have occurred in the first place, but what we find in Grimes's basement, it goes a long way to pushing the fast-forward button.

Monitors. Banks of them. Each screen home to a nightmare that had been pre-recorded or was live streaming.

Hence the merging of Jeramiah's gun and Grimes's frontal lobe.

But what comes next is new, and I admit to momentarily fighting the idea. I come to realize what I have known from the start, however: we'd never get them all. More to the point, we were smart enough to understand it was futile to even try.

So Jeramiah, he ensures we adapt. First embedding each recording of every one of the two hundred names we verify into an email and from Grimes's own IP address sends it not only to every family member he's able to find but to Culver PD as well.

Upheaval, thy name is years.

The end result even going national for a time.

But it's not enough. It never is. The suicides borne of the limelight we create, nor the convictions brought forth coming close to stopping the train this world rides upon.

Money.

Savior to the rich whenever they are caught out. Unfairly equipping the affluent with particular advantages that grant them the chance to circumvent a system broken beyond repair. Which brings us to Martin Loomis the third, but more so, his attorneys—the ones who ensure his sentence isn't just commuted by the end of his second trial but vacated entirely.

Act, and the universe responds.

Time to go to work.

Loomis was mine. The lawyers, Jeramiah's

Shiny when I lock on to him, wearing a blue speedo and in possession of two different kinds of six packs, he exudes trust fund baby, right down to his thick blonde curls. Under an umbrella for one, he sits alone in a lounge chair, drinks beer from a cooler, and watches everyone else as I watch him. Still glistening, I wait as he walks from the trunk of his Beemer to the driver's side door once he'd put the umbrella, cooler, and chair away. I open the van's sliding door abruptly, startling him, Loomis's large mouth a perfect wide O by the time the syringe is into his carotid. Done, he helps me in a way I least expected, falling forward instead of straight down. I make a mental note to thank him when he wakes.

Back at the Ronson house is a whole other story, and one where Jeramiah is already set up and waiting.

Same as Buchannan, the basement here had been sound-proofed years ago, holding many of the same armaments. What it lacked, however, was a White Room. Where such a room could exist sat black drum barrels, eleven in total, and adjacent to these ran workbenches that held a variety of tools: chainsaws, bone saws, axes, and hammers. Above these tools, I'd cut and taped to the wall articles that highlighted Loomis, his defence team, and the outcome of both trials. Did I expect anything to come of this? No. But they needed to see.

"I told you there was going to be a reunion," Jeramiah says. If they understood, their faces didn't show it. But gagged as they were, bound to chairs and under fluorescent light as they were, the Delucas never look away as they watch us first bind a still-unconscious Loomis to another chair and then turn said chair so everyone faced each other.

And I can't say why I did it, as I don't usually let them have a say, but something in the husband's eyes prompted me to take down his gag.

"You're the guy," he spits out, unafraid—one of the two options that generally presented itself in situations like this. Unlike his wife, he was still in his work clothes, the suit dark grey. It matched his hair. "I know you're the guy. Fuck, when they find you."

At first, I think he's on about Culver PD—that they'd finally decided there was someone out there exactly like me. But no, it wasn't the cops.

"I know who you mean, Deluca. I believe your wife here knows too. What I don't think you realize is we've taken on worse." It was the Armenians, of course, but I don't get to relay the information, not as Jeramiah, full arc, continues forward and, axe in hand, enters the top of Loomis's right knee with such force that some of the chair goes with it.

Loomis's head doesn't just rise up from his chest at this occurs, but *snaps* up, the veins on his neck the same as his eyes.

The leg falls to the right, the initial jet of blood surging far enough forward to reach Justine Deluca's skirt. Her eyes close when this happens, her head beginning to shake like a woman who feels she must be in a dream.

"It didn't have to be this way," I say and reapply Mark's gag. "And I think you know that. But that boy, he was eight."

I feel him stiffen, there as I'm down in his ear. I'd like to say it was because of what I'd said, but it's not, it's Jeramiah and how he'd switched from leg to speedo that held Deluca's attention. Fair enough, sure, as it was quite the show, but one that was far from over, even after Loomis's head is given flight.

"What I have a hard time reconciling is the tape. That's the thing." Were they listening? Did they understand? On some level, I'm sure they did, or were, but their eyes and the glazed look that had come over them led me to believe the percentage landed somewhere below the fifty percent mark. Didn't stop me from continuing, however. "Both of you saw it. Both of you watched what Loomis did. Despite this, despite having children of your own, you chose to defend him anyway."

It's not a coincidence we end up at the Ronson house. The drum barrels and the last time we'd used them coming to include men who needed a little extra time to contemplate what they'd done. Justine Deluca doesn't quite understand this, not even after she's placed in one. And I could have told her how I felt her children would be fine in the custody of her parents, but no, I choose to think of the boy instead. How Loomis not only ruined his body and life but how people like Mark and Justine Deluca seem unable to comprehend that defending the indefensible came with a price all its own. Especially when dealing with someone like me.

I look to Jeramiah. He looks to me.

"All right," I say. "Together, then."

And as I watch Justine Deluca's eyes close to the descending darkness, I lower the lid and lock it in place.

Universe or not, we finished the work.

OLD DOG, NEW TRICKS

The number eighty-eight sits in each corner of the bay windows on each side of the entrance to The Hair of The Dog. Inside, I'm greeted by the smell of stale beer, used cigarettes, and the ghost of something in-between.

"Not open until eleven, fella. Says so on the door you just walked through."

Dark oak and trimmed at the bottom in gold, the bar is to the left of me. Straight ahead, in front of three large swastika flags, stand two chest-high tables, and to the right of these, past a rectangle that opened to a kitchen, a row of six more. Not the largest watering hole I'd ever entered, but easily the stupidest.

I look to Randy and peg his thin mustache and ponytail as possible points of pride. It could have been the no shirt/leather vest combo too, but no, I stick with the tail.

"I read it, Randy. It's not your hours of operation I'm here to discuss. What I want is for you to get Papple on the phone. What I'd also like is for you to tell him two things. Tell him you want him to come here alone, and then tell him the person he's been looking for is done fucking around." It was true. All of it. Even if things finished contrary to how I wanted them to.

Randy stares at me, momentarily unsure, and as I turn back to lock the door, I mention it might also be wise if he ran a mop over the floor.

"Now just a—"

"The Arizona," I say. "Mention that too, Randy. Either way,

realize this is the last chance I'm going to give you."

Randy swallows. Randy reaches into his jeans. Randy heeds my advice.

John Papple was not good people. This is not to say I'm the opposite. I've just accepted the fact.

"And just who the fuck are you?" He's bigger than Randy, built, in boots and white jeans and sporting nails sharp as his cheekbones.

"Sit down," I say. "But first, tell your men coming up from the side of this building that if they want to live, it'd be wise to find their vehicles and head back the way they came."

Silence greets this. One second. Two.

"Who..."

"Last chance, John. Do I look like a man who cares to fuck around?"

John makes the call. John then takes a seat in front of me, his back to the swastika flags. Randy joins us, and it works in my favor that he picks the seat nearest his boss.

"I'll make it quick, John," I say and begin opening sugar packets two at a time and dumping their contents into the middle of the table. Randy protests this, of course, but I inform him there was, in fact, a method to my madness. I also mention my head and how I realize each of them wanted to put a bullet into it, but because I brought up Arizona, I'd granted myself this little reprieve.

"Takes some kind of balls to pull this kind—" I stop him there. I didn't want a discussion. Didn't want a *do you have any idea who I am?* Nor a *yeah, you and what army?* I only wanted him dead.

"I'll start by saying I'm tired. Neither of you knows why and neither of you cares. I get this. I do. But those films you've been making, they end today. They will not continue." They look at me, then they look at each other, and for a few seconds longer than I think it should last, I see the wheels and how they attempt to turn in their heads.

"And just how the fuck—" but the red dot that pops to life on Randy's forehead stops Papple mid query. I still answer, of course. I mean, it's the way these situations were played.

I spread my hand through the sugar on the table and even it out as best I can. I write FOLLOW THE CHILDREN into the granules and watch as each man follows my finger as I do. Did they understand? Could they? On some level, sure, but like my age and the options it has taken from me, they'd deny it for as long as their minds would allow.

"You have one on you too, John. But a smart guy like you, I think you already knew that. And this here, these words, it won't put an end to everything you've set in motion, but what it will do is ensure certain people start looking into parts of your life in ways they've yet to." I see it come together in his eyes. Not all of it, no, but enough for him to realize how he'd been caught.

"I'd consider yourselves lucky, too, as there was a time it wouldn't happen like this." True again, but I don't elaborate; don't divulge that chopping off heads from afar was an activity I was still getting used to.

I stand. I rise. Jeramiah and Ray taking their cue. The twin release of sniper rifles from two hundred yards away shattering the bay windows first and disintegrating skull bone second. The swastika flags behind the men dripping dirtbag by the time I've reached the door.

Not *exactly* the scenario I'd envisioned once we discovered what Papple and his crew were up to on that compound, but as large a problem as they'd become, I understood why Jeramiah thought it best we go this route. If anything, I owed him that much. His idea. His plan.

Culver PD would either run with what we'd given them or fumble the ball. I had my suspicions as to which.

Either way, the baton had been passed.

Either way, we prepared for war.

***

But war doesn't come, not how I imagined, and CCPD holds onto the ball.

It takes them weeks, sure, but by the end, Papple's compound is raided and the children found within are taken into custody. Nineteen becoming the number by the time everything is tallied. Children being exploited, not the clients and perps you see on video being escorted from the property. A deeper dive and one might suggest a type of cult had come into play along the way—the neo-Nazis that made up this particular organization, however, they do not bend to such an assessment.

Behind an armed gate, the main facility was pre-war, made of brick but run down and crumbling in more than a few places. Windows stood broken, glass like teeth, but more were boarded up and not very effective at that. Five portables, rectangular and grey, encircled the larger structure and from within these is where most of it went down—where they not only housed the children but trafficked and filmed in equal measure.

Large an operation as it was, guarded as it was, it still ate at me that we couldn't go at them like I wanted.

"Too much firepower, Bishop. Look at the pictures. It's not only machetes these guys are wearing." Jeramiah was right, of course, and from as close to the beginning as this went back. There was collateral damage to consider as well, and it's here as always that things fall apart; where, in fact, they began to change.

And admitting to it or not, the constant remained: I was not as young as I used to be.

"Doesn't mean we can't go at these fuckers from a different angle. Just means we might have to change the narrative is all." He pauses there, takes the extra second, and then looks up from the pictures of the compound that he'd taken himself. He smiles. I knew the look. But Jeramiah and his narrative—we'd played that game before. And although I'd understood where he was coming from, I still fought against the idea. What changes my mind? Papple's head, of course—how Jeramiah went and guaranteed its removal.

Fast forward through to the end of the events at the bar, the raid at the compound, and the eventual trials that come of it, we get to this morning, where a kind of epilogue is given life: where Papple's number two guy, a man named Cohen, in return for every dirtbag he flips on, is granted immunity.

"Time to go to work?" Jeramiah asks.

"Time to go to work," I respond.

He's heavyset, five ten, with a mustache and gut that were thicker than most. In the surveillance video, you can see him walking to and from the compound in dirty jeans, a cowboy hat, and a machete displayed over one big-boned hip. It's this particular bit of fashion sense that pulled at me—that I felt I'd seen the image before.

Three guesses as to where.

Naked except for a pair of grey boxers and a balaclava to cover his face, he and his gut are unmistakable. Hanging where I'd first seen it, on that same mound of hip, the machete is removed before he climbs on top of the girl.

"I had a speech planned, Lono. I did. Me going on about how you must have been pretty pleased with yourself, coming out of that bust like you did." He looks at me, his eyes on fire. But the fat man's sweating too, his hands in chains above him as his boots just barely brush the concrete. "Thing is, Lono, I want you to know I was pleased too. I mean, if you hadn't done what you did to save your own ass, what happens next, it never occurs."

I bring up the machete. Not his, of course, but one quite similar. I turn it. His eyes never leaving the blade. And I'm selfish here. I admit that. As some part of me still didn't want things to change, not even here, after everything; didn't want to admit I was hampered by what I'd already been hampered by. But Cohen, part of what I would come to think of as the old way, I use him as I needed to, bridging what came before to what I could no longer deny.

It means I end him proper.

More to the point: I make it last.

ARCS OF DESCENT

Gentlemen! Good morning! I trust you both slept well. Well, sleep is an operative word right now, isn't it? Yeah, that cocktail we gave each of you, it *can* kick you in the head pretty fuckin' hard. All good, though. Take a moment, acclimate yourself. And yes, this warehouse *is* cold this time of day. Doesn't help you're in your birthday suits either, but hey, that's neither here nor there. Or is it?

On a sidenote: Jonathan, dude, a little manscaping goes a long way, buddy. It also makes the size of one's hammer appear larger in the long run. I'm speaking from experience here, Jonathan, so the eye fucking, there's really no need. What we're born with, it's genetics is all. I mean, look at Wayne here—pretty sure that thing is close to having its own fucking solar system.

But I digress...

So, you're naked: check. You're also secure, gagged, and positioned in the shape of an X and beside one another on a concrete floor of an undisclosed location that neither of you remembers being brought to. Means we should probably get to the why of the situation then.

What? You thought I was going to leave you in the dark?

People. People, people, people.

If I haven't already made this abundantly clear, let me do so now: I'm the talker of the group. Always have been. Always will be. Long after you two are dead and gone and long after others have taken your place.

We good? Up to speed? Yeah, I thought that might do it. Anyway...

Jonathan Kynard, male, age twenty-two. Wayne Fenlon, also male, also aged twenty-two. At age seventeen, however, you two shitbirds decide you're going to pull some shit and fuck anything that comes of it. I pretty much nail things there? No? Hmm. Maybe I start someplace else then. Maybe I tell you how people such as yourselves get radared by people like us in the first place. Sounds about fair. I mean, it runs along the same kind of line.

It deals with a man named Rider and the death of *his* family, if you must know. Where he loses his mother and sister, though, the man whose life you two destroy loses his wife and daughter. Oh, you suddenly seeing the parallel, Wayne? Of course you are. Your bladder too by the looks of things. But that's to be expected, right? Once you realize this is, in fact, the last place you'll ever see? Yeah, you're getting it now, Wayne. Oh yes, indeed. And would you look at that: Jonathan here has gone and seen the light as well! No crossing streams though, boys. I mean, what would the neighbors think?

Now, where was I? Oh yes. So Rider loses his family, and this devastation, it changes the man. Putting him on a collision course that involves men like me, men like you, and if I'm honest, many a shitbird between.

Bottom line is this: he's attempting to balance the carnage you and people like you create. He's not attempting to hold the line, though. No, he's chosen to obliterate it. You two but twin dirtbags in a long line of the same.

But wait, there's more!

This man, Rider, he's had help throughout the years. Men like yours truly, yes, but men in positions of power as well. Men who aid in getting us to within spitting distance of pieces of garbage like you.

And no, it's not just anyone they let near juvenile records. No, those records are sealed. But if you were a detective, say, and one who doesn't mind breaking the rules for what certain like-minded individuals see as the greater good, then fellas, yeah, you guessed it: you'd be fucked but good.

Means we don't care that you were underage when you threw that cinderblock from that overpass, Wayne. Means we don't care you were right there beside him, Jonathan. What we do care about, however, is the windshield that cinderblock entered and the persons beyond.

It created a mini bomb, in effect—the speed at which that minivan was traveling and the arc of descent you placed that brick on. And yes, I know you know this; it was repeated ad nauseum at your trials. But gentleman, bottom line again, we just don't think you care—that you never have.

I mean, that cinderblock sheared off half of Doreen Sweeny's face before destroying her left shoulder and, because physics and momentum are nothing if not steadfast bastards, sends it back into the car seat holding nine-month-old Ava Sweeny.

Destruction on top of destruction on top of destruction.

This is even before I mention the father, Liam Sweeny, and his subsequent suicide. This falls squarely onto both of your shoulders as well. Your actions and what they create—the entire reason we are here today. It also means the cinderblocks on this catwalk, yeah, they're upon it for the exact reason you think they are. And just so you know, I walked all forty-two of these bad boys up here myself. No, no, please, your struggling is thanks enough. Seriously, I take it as a sign you understand. It's not enough, of course, but progress is progress, right? What? My goggles? Yeah, bought 'em just special. Why? Oh, come on now, boys, I think you know why. All right, I'll humor you. Two reasons: your heads, more so your torsos, they are not my intended targets. Not at first, anyway. And second, well, second is because bone fragments sometimes have minds of their own.

And yes, I realize the height of this catwalk is a little bit less than the actual height of that overpass, but gentleman, the donuts I'm about to make, I don't think it much matters. We good then? All questions answered? Okay. Bear with me then. Or at least hold still. These old arms of mine, they ain't what they fuckin' used to be.

NOT IN A THOUSAND LIFETIMES

Hightower may have killed Ray, but the names we pull from the man after the fact go a long way in the end. Never equaling what was taken, no, but I choose to believe the good it allowed us to achieve—it accounted for something.

"You see this," Jeramiah says, holding Hightower's detached leg by the ankle, from the knee down, out over the incinerator. We're at the place on Buchannan and, vertical, Hightower is down to his boxers and strapped to a surgical table. One, now that I think about it, we never fully release him from. Not alive, anyway. "It's just the beginning, Hightower. *Bet* on it."

It was true. Every word. The other leg taken from Hightower in front of a full-length mirror so the man could witness the bone saw and how it was designed to work. To ensure this transpires, I keep the man drugged and hooked to IVs and add both a colostomy bag and catheter but in the end decide his eyelids brought a type of interference he didn't deserve.

That was summer.

And the names Hightower produces, they were as far and wide as I imagined they'd be. From client lists to a production team to recordings similar to the one that took April from the world. My sister going out not just hard but in ways that removed dignity and humanity from an equation that never should have been.

We get to work.

We track. We watch. We capture and destroy.

And by late fall, Hightower finds himself down to only an

arm and a pair of stubs that used to be thighs. I remove his birthmark as well, the stubbled cheek it'd been a part of since conception a concave crater once I'd gotten to the roots.

"I know you want it to be over, Neal. I see it. But like I told you at the start: you shouldn't have come at me from the side. You should have taken me head-on."

True again. And the man lasts longer than either Jeramiah or I thought possible, our total time together coming in at just under a year. I'd like to say we found he had a brother along the way as well, or a father, or someone as close to him as Ray had been to me. We don't, though, not how I'd have liked. In the end, my version of a death by a thousand cuts proving the most fulfilling response to Hightower and what he and his men had done to Ray.

I'd like to say there was more. I would. But I can't. All I could do was burn what remained. All I could do was continue the work.

And work we did. Doubling down almost, as I'd come to rely more on weapons than my hands. A lifetime of battle catching up and invading parts of my body in ways I could no longer deny. But we go on, push forward, and then Batista re-enters the frame.

"What kind of trouble?" I explain to Jeramiah what Batista tells me. It involved a night nurse, but one who wasn't so much a caregiver as he was a predator—and one now loose in the retirement home destined to become John's last-known address. Jeramiah goes to work; digs into a man named Gish, Robert J; finds the man had been just as busy at his previous place of employment. Nothing sticks to him, however, and in the end the man is only asked to move on, allowing Gish to turn up where he had, his dick most nights into a senior who'd be hard-pressed to remember the event.

"Hey, old man," I say as I walk into the room. On the far side of him, in line with his head, a dialysis machine beeped softly, the intravenous lines he was tethered to pulling tight as he sat up. Even through the beard, his scars remained. Newer were the liver spots that covered him now, more than they had back in the day.

"I could say the same." I smile. Batista, in return, musters up one of his own. It'd been over a decade since the big man retired, fifteen years since Harrison Garrett took parts of his face off in strips.

We reminisce. Batista telling me of his cabin and a life devoid of the things we'd done. "We did some good, though," he says. "I know we did." And then he pauses, staring out the window. It could have been the cancer. It could have been the Alzheimer's. I choose to believe it was neither.

Before I leave, he tells me what he'd wanted since before he even made the call. "Ensure he suffers. That's all I ask."

Then as well as now, he didn't have to.

But I fail here, Gish so worked up that I might shoot him in the face that I feel his face could be the only way things played out.

No. Just please...not my face. Not my face! My mother, man!

And had Batista been there, I believe he would have understood. However, it's what Jeramiah recovers from a second laptop that awakens my rage. Unlike Hightower, Gish *did* have a brother, and one with a record longer than my days are bleak.

Like sand through an hourglass—these, the days of my life.

Where the older Gish had been an Ichabod Crane–type who wore Buddy Holly frames, Velencio Gish was thicker in the middle, with a sloped forehead and straight, corn yellow teeth. He also preferred the opposite of what walked the halls and sat in the breakfast nooks of where Batista ended up.

All told, it was enough to make you scream.

For Velencio, we return the favor, but only after we come up to him from behind and find him passed out in a chair.

On the TV is an infomercial turned low, and beside the man's tattered La-Z-Boy sat a collection of drained aluminum. To the right of him and against a peeling wall sat a half-folded kitchen table and upon it a mountain of unfolded clothes. Behind this stretched a couch clearly being used for a bed. In front of it and on a leg-taped coffee table stood more beer cans, some fallen, more crushed, all of them dusted in flecks of cigarette ash.

Jeramiah steps to one side. I, the other.

"Velencio," Jeramiah says. "Yo, Velencio." But it takes a third nudge until the man starts, his stained smiley-face T-shirt straightening as he attempts to get himself vertical.

"Don't bother," I say and introduce the butt end of the sawed-off to some of the yellow that occupied the man's mouth. It brought red into the picture, sure, and almost like it'd been planned.

Back at Buchannan, he's up in chains and the blood is a dried curtain on his chin by the time he comes to. "You don't know me, Velencio. But know I knew your brother. Unlike him, we're going to make this last."

But I can't, not after the first ten swings. His ribs are close to pulp, sure, and he slips in and out of consciousness with every second blow, but my stamina deserts me, and again I find myself passing the baton.

Jeramiah steps forward, plants himself, and as I hear the parts I couldn't break begin to shatter, I think of Hightower. But then I think of Ray. Followed by Batista. How each man helped me in ways I could never repay, not in a thousand lifetimes. Each of them no longer a part of what we do, but even gone, a part of the process regardless.

"For Ray," Jeramiah says.

"For John," I reply.

Behind the gag, Velencio screams.

FATBOY SLIM

It didn't have to be this way, but looking back, maybe it did. Either way, what we'd been doing was always going to attract attention, missing bodies or otherwise. Careful though we'd been, it meant things were bound to catch up with us in time. It came to involve a type of hubris too, and if I'm going to admit the fact, I also have to acknowledge my awareness of it. It created a balance/counterbalance effect, however, and since I'm in a giving mood, one that helped me more than it hindered me.

Brings us to Fatboy Slim, or rather, Rudy Dodge, and the Navarro-Grimes recordings—the gift that kept on giving. Tried, found guilty, and incarcerated for his crimes, Dodge spends nineteen months behind bars before he's released for good behavior. Translation: the penal system remained the joke it was, broken and beyond repair even before I put on the badge.

Nineteen months for destroying the life of a five-year-old. Nineteen months, and the man had been set free.

"It's off Henderson, up behind the canal. I swung by yesterday. Three exits. Front, side, and rear. I suggest we go in through the backyard." Jeramiah puts on his windbreaker. He's thicker now, thicker than his father had been. He retained his old man's eyes, however, small and oil-like. It paired well with the crooked smile.

"The rear it is, then." I agree and start the van. Fully engaged, it's during the first of two drive-bys that I take notice of each parked vehicle and then the blue Caprice and sun-glassed occupants within. Could be nothing. Could be something. I note the two men either way. Inside is a whole other story, and one Rudy Dodge is only too happy to tell.

"They know I didn't do it, man. Tape or no tape. And you know how I know? I'm right here, man. They made me a free man." Jeramiah had him sitting on a leather couch that had seen better days, arms zip-tied behind him. In grey sweats, soft in the middle, and sporting more stubble than actual hair, he looked at me the only way people with a wandering eye can.

Something seemed off.

Maybe it was the car, that was a given. But the ankle monitor Dodge wore, Jeramiah's guy hadn't mentioned it. It brought scenarios into play, and interactions my mind was predicting by the second.

"Gag him," I tell Jeramiah, and once he had, I bring a finger to my lips and then hook a thumb back toward the kitchen and the way we came. Back in the van, I relay my suspicions. "Only one way to find out," he says. I pull back onto Dodge's street, passing the Caprice first and the front of Dodge's bungalow second. At the stop sign, the Caprice starts up, pulls out, and the feeling I'd had doesn't just double, but triples.

Someone was onto us.

Someone *knew*.

"I need you," I say to Ray and then explain. I also tell him one thing had to happen before the other, and then I cut the call.

We drive. Not the speed limit, just over. Jeramiah watching our pursuers from the side-view mirror.

"Four cars back and in line. You think law enforcement or Armenian?" For truth, the Armenians never crossed my mind. But blue? Blue I could do. I tell him as much.

"Makes me think they don't have much to go on," I add. "If they did, I don't think we'd have made it out of the house." I drive on, take an off-ramp, hit a Dunkin' Donuts drive-thru, loop back onto the highway, and keep heading east. Thirty minutes on, I turn back toward Culver and the setting sun, hoping I'd timed things right.

I hear Ray honking before I see him, his headlights coming off the off-ramp behind us and crossing all four lanes in one go. His van gets the Caprice's attention, has to, but alas, no cherries. Curiouser and curiouser. And good ole Ray, he reads the room, and in an instant, commits himself, pulling back from in front of the Caprice and lining up to its rear.

I take the moment.

Pick my place.

And as I watch Ray come up alongside the Caprice's right side, I cut all the way over and take the ramp. I hear horns and tires, but I see no Ray. No Caprice.

We drive on into the night. It was time to make another call.

Batista gets back to me in under forty-eight hours. "Called in a few favors here, Bishop. Just thought you'd want to know." I appreciated it and told the man so. What I didn't tell him was that he was missed. He'd earned his retirement, from the badge as well from what he helped me accomplish on the side. No need to muddy the frame.

"I hope that cabin has a nice view at least." He chuckled and said it did, and I swear I could hear his smile spreading on the other end of the phone. What I couldn't deny, however, was the change in his voice. Made me think I owed him more than my life. Possibly my soul.

Like always, he gets to business and chooses the long way. Many of the instances I can pull up at will, seeing the blood we'd spilled and more times than not, each and every body part the liquid came from.

"But it's this calling card you and the kid began," he says. "This is what's created your jackpot." Did I hear an actual shoe drop as he says this? No, but it took me back to the hubris I mentioned, the balance, and how I now saw it for everything it was.

A message, sure, and one that started with a reverend named Ducard and how Jeramiah left it in stark letters on the man's living room wall.

FOLLOW THE CHILDREN.

Ever since, we'd run with it, and seeing where we were now, perhaps a bit too much.

Maybe a lot too much.

But self-inflicted or not, it created something too, or at least pointed certain people in the direction I felt we couldn't go. Was it worth it? I'd like to say it was, but no, I can't. I'm a different breed of monster is all, and broken down, just a better version of the same type of hate. Saving lives, though noble, had become by definition a byproduct of what I needed to do and nothing more. Didn't make things better, nor did it make them worse. It did what it always did, it remained what it would always be: me burning as many of them as I could and stacking their bodies like wood.

"It's a thick file too, Rider. Some of the info going back to our time together. Back before Alex and Mapone."

"No names, I take it?"

"You think we'd be talking if they did?" He was right, of course, but same as my anger, old habits died hard. "It hasn't gone federal yet either, but a statewide BOLO levels you up all the same. Might be time to slow it down again is what I think. If anything, at least stop signing walls." I smiled at that. How could I not? Batista, a man as predictable as they came; a man who continued to wear his heart where men like us should not.

"I'll take it under advisement, John," I say and picture him there in his cabin man attire, there on his phone. I ignore the scars in my memory, the ones inflicted upon him by a madman who no longer breathed. I chose to envision him in full beard, six three head to boot, and the man who in the end helped me save the world the only way I knew how.

"Thanks for the intel."

I'd told Ray to remove Dodge's ankle monitor before he grabbed the man and transported him to the Buchannan house. Did Dodge know, though? That was the million-dollar question. I let him sweat it out in the basement for the duration, including the time it took for Batista to gather what he could and for Ray to deal with the vans.

"Did they tell you anything, that's what I'm trying to piece together. Or did they just hang you out there like a piece of meat?" Sweatshirt failing to do its job, he's fully awake now, his one eye aimed directly at me, the other flaring to the right. I hear Jeramiah take a seat behind us both, Dodge bound to a chair himself. "It's not unheard of, though, and I've seen men receive less time for the same offence. Still, would they trust you?" On the one hand, I believed they would. Could see how it might be plotted; that the trail of bodies being left with the same message scrawled at more than a few scenes would act as a boon if not an incentive for any cop who broke the case. On the flipside, I'd experienced firsthand how cops could turn a blind eye to helping their own.

That's what decided it, I think; how Culver PD mishandled April's and my mother's murders all those years ago. No rhyme. No reason. Just playing a hunch that they had, in fact, kept Dodge in the dark. It brings Jeramiah to his feet and then from his pocket a knife. Opening it, an audible click as unmistakable as the sun fills the room.

"Can't remember the last time I took a man's eyes, Rudy," he says. "And a wandering one at that." Rudy responds in ways any man in his position would, but his body couldn't buck, not bound as it was.

Would it change things? For a bit, yes, but like every time I'd gone to ground, the message would return. There was a certain group of neo-Nazis up the line, you see, and a future that involved a man who fancied parkas, earplugs, and power buffers in ways you weren't supposed to. FOLLOW THE CHILDREN would never be used as vigorously as it had, no, but as I also mentioned: old habits, they died hard.

Little did I know, so would I.

HUMBLE BEGINNINGS

"You right-handed or left-handed?" He looks to me, up from the chair he's bound to. The wood is mahogany—old, thick, and matching the desk I'm leaning against. Stout juts his chin to the right, the sweat dripping from his goatee adding to the dampness already home to his crotch.

I cut the zip tie that binds his right hand to the chair.

"And you?" I say, turning my attention to the other piece of shit, McDonough. The thicker man looks to his right hand as well, but as he does, Ray re-enters the office. Like me, he's still wearing the Kevlar. Unlike me, he comes bearing gifts: a gas can in each of his gloved hands.

"I see you've started without me." In a way I had, but not how one might think. I'm young here, no longer part of the CCPD, and at a time in my life where failure and I had yet to fuck one another. It meant Jeramiah was still years into the future, Batista still retained the parts of his face he'd eventually lose, and Ray, well, Ray was still six feet instead of five.

"Just awaiting your return," I say and feel the metal hit the desk.

Ray sucks his teeth. "That's why these two are going to love you, Bishop. You're inclusive in what you do, never failing to leave anyone out of the process." He's fucking with them now, and the show, it wasn't new. It's how Ray's always been, war, post-war, or otherwise.

I finish my business with McDonough, freeing the hand he'd

motioned to. We're in the man's own office, surrounded by pin-up posters, a couple of filing cabinets topped with liquor bottles, and a small beige couch that had seen better days. Through venetian blinds to the right of Stout, I take in Culver Bay, the docks, and the purple sky above them both. A storm was coming. For some, it was already here.

"Each of you are going to list as many people as you can. Men who could sit in those very chairs and I'd have a hard time spotting the difference." I had their attention. Of course I did. It's the way this game was played. Home to a set of rules I'd been forced to understand.

"Whoever gives me the highest number of shitbirds, you are the one who walks. Not forever. Just today. Until Ray and I here come looking for you again." If they were smart, they'd picture using that time to either come at me themselves or hightail it the fuck out of Dodge.

It's what the man in front of them hoped they'd believe, anyway.

I hand them pens and clipboards.

They write. Stout faster than McDonough. This surprises me, even though it shouldn't have. Not because human trafficking is a billion-dollar industry, but because dirty cops have always been a beast all their own.

Goatee still dripping, Stout gestures through the gag. "You sure?" He nods. I take the clipboard. Read it. Look to McDonough. "You need more time?" He shakes his head, his eyes like O's, and then he begins to openly weep. I nod to Ray.

From the small duffel, he removes goggles and places them on the bald man's head, taking and then handing me the clipboard in the process.

"You're thinking, 'Why the goggles,' am I right?" And Ray, as he likes to do when we get to this part, he hunkers down and places his hands upon McDonough's knees. "It's because feeling what's about to occur is only half of what people like you deserve. You need to see."

Protests come next—a type of pleading from both men, the kind that each of them would withhold from others without a thought.

Did it change things? Would it?

No. And then McDonough is drowning in fuel, his clothes hungry for the liquid. Ray empties the can, shakes it, then switches it for the full one. He sets it a few feet in front of the man. My turn. I push Stout closer to that gas can, ensuring he would accept the full brunt of what was to come.

Neither was ever leaving this office alive, no matter how much they wanted to believe in what I told them. Part of them probably knew that, but still, I'd never ask.

I'd lost my mother. I'd lost my sister. I'd one day lose a leg. But here now, back at the start, I was not yet the monster I needed to become.

The fire spreads fast, the explosion coming faster. From the passenger seat of the van, I pull the names from the clipboards— names I did not have at the start of the day. Ray smiles. I nod.

Time to go to work.

Look, I'm not going to sugarcoat things. These overhead lights, Danny, this basement, it's the last place you're ever going to see. And everything that's planned, it's going to happen right over there, and you are going to feel every last bit of it before we dump you in that hole. Call it a threat, call it a promise, call it me predicting the goddamn future, I really don't give a shit. What you did, Danny, what you got away with, in my opinion, it deserves all this and more.

It's not my opinion that matters, though—I'm just the guy before the guy.

What, you thought this was a two-player game?

Danny.

Danny, Danny, Danny.

Seeing as we still have some time to burn, I'll start at the beginning then.

Your name, Danny, it was part of a list—a list extracted from men much like yourself. Not in appearance, no, but in level of dirtbag. The one guy, a dirty cop, you don't know, but McDonough, yeah, you and he had history. Not anymore, of course.

Man went up in flames, Dan. Yessir. It ended with an explosion too, but it's really your name and others on that list that bring us to you gagged and tied to that chair. And I'm not going to lie—it *was* difficult tracking you down. Side quest after side quest after goddamn fucking side quest if I'm honest.

Don't look at me like that, Dan. We found you in a stained wifebeater asleep on a couch in front of a PS3, for Christ's sake. I know you know what a side quest is.

But all right, you look at me like you are a moron, I'm going to treat you like one.

These pit stops, the ones on our way to you—they involve a very particular man. A man who I've been helping for a little while now. It goes back to that list and the other names upon it, the ones above yours, and how it created certain opportunities by attacking them in the order in which they were written down. This man's name, Danny? Rider. Sound familiar?

Yeah, I thought it might.

Anyway, we get to about halfway down this list your name is on, on to a man named Terrance, and this Terrance, he points us in the direction of a man named Toomey.

Lot of names to keep track of, I know.

Lemme try and make it easier for you.

Don't gimme that face, Dan. Seriously. You have no sway here, no play. You drugged and raped your wife and monetized that shit. That you only served six years for what you did is what irks us the most, I suppose. Can you spell travesty, Dan? I sure as fuck can. But timeline-wise, it *did* coincide with McDonough giving you up, so maybe, just maybe, I shouldn't be looking a gift horse in the mouth as unkindly as I am.

Anyway. Where was I?

Oh, yes. Rider. If I'm honest again, he's rage and anger and a man who clearly has issues. His mother and sister were murdered, Dan, the sister being raped by six men in masks before she succumbs. Like you, however, certain men made available for public consumption the tape that depicted April Rider's demise.

The picture beginning to get a little clearer now, Dan?

Anyway, the list, those opportunities, one of them being Toomey and how Rider takes this man out with a rocket launcher, it's how this, a much more intimate setting, has come to pass. It means a man like Rider and what he's attempting to do, it can only be done out in the open for so long without attracting unwanted attention.

It's why you and he and the tools upon those workbenches over there are about to get as comfortable as you got with your unconscious wife. Consent, violation, and how one is meant to conduct themselves upon this planet is going to be explored, in other words. This little refresher—

Well, would you look at that. Man's as silent as he is big, ain't he? Not as big as Batista, but still. Anyway, that's my cue, Dan. I'd like to say it's been fun, but no, you deserve everything this man is about to take from you. Everything he's about to remove.

If you're lucky, Dan, he may even let you scream.

There are truths to this world. Most are what they should be: universal. Others, however, can be circumvented, allowing men like me to not only flourish, but thrive.

It means the list of names we pull from McDonough and a bent cop named Stout works better than I'd hoped. Not perfect by any means, as two of the nine proved beyond our reach, and it still takes close to a year to track each of them down.

"This is going to end how you think it will, Paul. I believe you know this. The question I want you thinking about, though, is this: will Ray here start cutting something other than that rope before it does?"

Ray sucks his teeth and hunkers down in front of the older man's head. The tanned face looking up at Ray's angular one is stubbled, sweating, and sporting two veins competing for dominance across a forehead that, if pressed, could house about twenty-seven more. "Anything! I'll do anything!" Of course he would. Strung up as he was, up and over the end of an old silo, tends to do that, I'd found. Especially where people like Paul J. Garth were concerned.

Full disclosure: this early into things, I'd only used this property one other time. But the pulley system Garth found himself dangling from? Built and erected by Ray himself. Wouldn't be the last time Ray built me something either, most of these future upgrades coming to reside within the basement of a very particular house.

"I'm a simple man, Paul," Ray says, and taking the man by his right ear, pulls him back in past the edge. The breeze freshens here, and the sun, it has almost put itself to bed. "Like Bishop said, I believe in what we're doing—that this has to be done. It means I do feel like something more is required before we watch your bones erupt from your skin, but instead, Paul, I'm going to make you a deal."

"Anything! Anything!"

But Paul, he doesn't care for what he hears. Neither do I. Not really. But things need to be said aloud sometimes. Like memories, they need to exist.

"Eleven pounds is what that child weighed, Paul. You admit that, I let you keep this ear." But Paul continues in his ways. His denial coming in head shakes, body bucks, and deep-throated moans not many men get to hear. Some spittle too, of course, traveling far up the man's cheeks but alas, never reaching his eyes. Yet he would not mention the microwave. Nor the meth he copped to in his original statement—the one where he gave up his thoughts on how he knew his then-girlfriend had been holding out on him.

It's unfortunate. All of it. And as I look to Ray, to the Ray of my past, his head still intact and unblemished by the machetes that would come to remove it, I see he's reached the same conclusion. And I'd like to say it was all Garth's doing, but I can't. Not how I'd like.

It was me, what I was; what I'd been forced to become.

I'd grown accustomed to it. Perhaps I even craved it. Making me no better than the men I had already ruined and the ones I'd yet to. But it did something else as well, even way back then. It allowed me to function in a world where as much as I fought to believe otherwise, certain truths remained as ignored as they were hidden.

I was done observing rules that benefited those who did not deserve them, in other words.

I was done leaving messages behind.

And as I cut through the rope connecting Garth to the world, I take a moment—not only to watch and listen to how the concrete destroys him, but to realize I'd not only embraced what I'd become, but that I enjoyed it. And that back then, same as now, I wouldn't change a thing.

I was what I needed to be. I *remain* what I need to be.

I would burn them all.

FEEDING THE MACHINE

I'll admit to becoming more inventive with how I'd chosen to approach certain scenarios along the way. Would I change this? No, I can't say I would. Patterns emerged, of course, and decapitation, I'll admit, it was never my first choice when attempting to rid this world of people who weren't really people at all. Once I realized how instrumental this particular method could be at extracting information, though—this is when the game not only changed for the better but upgraded itself to a level I never could have foreseen. Where the bodies we begin to stack became both a means to an end as well as a type of leverage that has yet to fail.

I'd like to say it was what came of the exchange too, and how more times than not it would arc like ribbon through the air, but no, I'd come to realize it was more the pieces of vertebrae and how Jeramiah liked to kick at the coated bone with the toes of his boots in front of whoever else was joining us at the time.

Everything I wanted to hear was then spoken, of course. Accompanied by a stutter most times, sure, but spoken all the same.

Like now, for instance.

More muscle than fat, Ippolito struggles to process what he'd just seen; watching me as I remove my prosthetic from atop the shovel, my last heel stomp producing from the man beneath me the aforementioned vertebrae and blood. I watch in real time as his face drops all traces of color as his gaze stops and sticks upon the slick expanding toward him.

"I've never been a man who tends to fuck around, Curtis. You and Bobby here, I think you understand that now. Well, you do anyway."

"It happens at Arnold's! They use the basement below the bar! Please, I don't want my head cut off. Please don't cut my head off!"

But we would cut his head off. We wouldn't remove him from his sitting position to achieve this outcome, however. No, his position in the chair would remain. The instrument of his death *would* change though—no shovel into the hollow of this man's neck, no. Now it would be Jeramiah and how from behind he raises his machete above the bound man's neck. Down and through, stuck and then unstuck, it takes four more passes until this head hits the concrete and manages to roll and then stop within inches of the one already occupying the basement floor.

I look from one head to the other and then back to Jeramiah. Ippolito's bound torso continues spasm, to spurt, and Jeramiah's smile, it incorporates everything I knew it would.

Experience, it's more than a teacher.

It's a goddamn machine.

"You want to live, you kept those hands topside, fella." Batista doesn't raise the sawed-off or his voice when he says this but expresses business all the same. The bearded man behind the bar sees things differently from the big man, however, and as his face exits the back of his skull, it proves the brain cells he'd possessed were far from what he needed them to be.

A type of pandemonium attempts to rise at this, of course, but both Ray and Jeramiah are ready, each man as well-versed in the act of crowd control as the other, especially when sawed-offs were involved.

The men in their sights understand things in a heartbeat, either sliding back onto their stools or moving back and around a pool table that had seen better days. The air not only thick in the moment but full of tobacco as well.

To my right stood the jukebox, its plug still in my hand. On my left, past varying sizes of confederate flags under glass, was an emergency exit that had already been wedged from the outside. In front of me: the bar. Beyond it, a mirror backsplash and bottles now peppered by blood and pieces of a man who would never again see.

"Now that we really have your attention, I think it's time we get to know one another." They look to me, all eleven of them, but not one of them responds. Men in trucker hats, men in flannel overcoats and jeans, men who in two decades time would be the type to have stickers on the bumpers of their trucks that claimed a reality TV star had been hand-picked by God. "But don't worry, I'll go first." No applause greets this, of course, but fear does, leading me to believe I had their undivided attention. I was wrong, sure, but a man should always dream.

The skinny one in leather, Daniels, he feels he has something to say. I disagree and hold up one gloved hand. Better than the man who'd never serve him alcohol again, he gets my meaning. The man on the stool beside Daniels, however…

"Do you have any idea…"

But we did have an idea. Many, in fact. Jeramiah, though, and much like Batista in front of him, he was having none of it. Explaining things not quite how the detective had, not so far north, but he ends up finding bone regardless.

Clad in checkered flannel and sporting a nose closer to the sun than most, the man falls from his stool and grabs at the place his left knee once was. His wailing is monstrous, primal, but over before it really even begins—Jeramiah's sawed-off against and then through the man's attempt at a beard in the blink of an eye. I wince at the discharge again, as do many others in the bar. Gunshot far louder than portrayed in movies and TV.

"You will listen to what this man has to say," Jeramiah states, half turning toward the right to address the majority of them. "That's what's happening here. You don't, it does nothing but give me a reason. Go on, give me a fuckin' reason." Not exactly like Batista, no, and I've mentioned this before, but Jeramiah, he comes awfully damn close.

I look down to what's left of the man he'd chosen to destroy and then up and over the ten of them who remained.

Justice, it has never been pretty.

Not when dealing with men such as these.

"Bigger operation than normal is all I'm saying, Bishop" He wasn't wrong, but Ray, more than any of them, he knew the drill. It's not that he was attempting to stop things either, only that caution would be required. I didn't disagree.

"On paper, it looks legit," I say but offer what Batista has relayed. "But there's a silent partner. It's not much, but it's enough. We've worked off less."

"Tell me something I don't know," and then he smiles. A small joke, sure, but if I'm anything, it's a creature of habit. A man of ritual. Embracing what I have in ways that I must.

"Time to go to work?"

He smiles again. "Time to go to work."

I tell them about how we'd heard rumblings of a service—that most of their names had been found upon a list. What I don't mention is the link. Dirtbags this world would be hard-pressed to miss. They look at each other, these men in work boots and flannel, these pieces of shit in trucker hats who sported wallets connected to chains, but as they light cigarette after cigarette, it's the bar's dark wood flooring that's suddenly the most interesting place of all.

"This place, what goes on down below, it may sound like it's the entire reason we're here, but it's not. This place, it has a benefactor. One of you is going to give me his name." True. All of it. Everything we'd accomplished in the last few months culminating in this moment, this time, to where, if I'm honest, I was about to find out that the past was not only about to destroy me but that it was about to swallow me whole.

It meant an enemy I hadn't foreseen was about the enter the fray.

The enemy? He was me.

Batista adjusts his chest plate, steps forward, and motions to the skinny piece of shit closest to him. "Up," he says, and once the man does, adds, "all of you."

Jeramiah and Ray take their cue and begin corralling the others. Ray following up alongside the pool table and Jeramiah out from his left. Single file they fall in line and make their way toward Batista, the bar, and the dimly lit alcove behind it. Well-traveled, they knew the way, every goddamn one of them.

I stop Ray as he begins his descent down the stairs. "Do me a favor," I say.

"Name it."

"Get me the axe."

Four against ten. I liked those odds. We'd rallied against worse, sure, but really, it was never going to be a fair fight. Not with sawed-offs and an axe.

"Some of you will attempt to run when this begins," I say but leave the axe at my side. "It's only natural. You want to live. You have forfeited this right, however, and being down here as we are, I believe the majority of us already understand this." Most give their eyes to this floor now, others openly weeping while a good number of them felt I could be killed by looks alone. Jeramiah flanks me while Batista flanks him. Ray is to my left, a long gun in his hands now, up and against his shoulder.

The basement holds better light than the narrow stairwell we descended and is larger than the bar above, full of kegs placed under shelves that backed onto concrete walls. Jars of pickled eggs, sausages, and liquor of every conceivable kind sit upon these shelves. Beyond these shelves, however, is the room that brings us together today. The one from the video that started this all. Clearly an addition, it had been built into and expanded beyond the original foundation.

"That room behind you, you're going to tell us who financed it. The person who you send what you record." It was always going to be this way. I shouldn't say always, though, as there have been times that situations don't go according to plan. Alex comes to mind, for one. Mapone, another. But here, now near the end, it was clear a push would be required.

I raise the axe and grab it by the neck. It does two things at once. One is a bonus, and the dampness I watch descend down the closest pair of jeans is as satisfying as the first fifty times I'd seen it occur. The other is Jeramiah and how in a heartbeat he has the shortest dirtbag by the back of his hair.

"It didn't have to be this way," he says, pulling the man forward, toward me, then forcing him to his knees. "For any of you." Batista moves close, as does Ray, alert and as ready as they needed to be.

I look down to the man, his thin face shaking in ways I'd seen before. Snot bubbles out from his nose, and as many of them do, he tries his best to explain why his life is worthy of being spared.

It's enough. As ever, it's enough. And the axe doesn't catch him as square as I wanted but high up under his right eye as he attempts to evade. The basement floods with screams, the "tunk" that came and the image they were processing too much for most of them to accept. It opens the gate and not one but two of them try to bolt. Batista and Ray take them out at the knee. The one falls into my boot, there as I'm removing the axe, but he's too preoccupied with his shattered bone to do anything of consequence.

"Kincaid! His name is Kincaid!"

I hear it, but I don't want to hear it. The moment it's said, my recklessness barrels up through the decay of my past and is exposed for what it was: for what I would spend the rest of my life atoning for.

My biggest regret. My greatest mistake.

Kincaid.

And yes, leaving messages as I had felt like the right thing to do at the time, but no, it had been wrong in too many ways to count. I know this now. I've known it for years. Evolving, transforming, and emerging into everything I'd chosen to destroy.

Mistakes, yeah, I've made a few.

But this is the moment I'm made aware. In this basement, in front of these men.

I could say I'd taken limbs from the man, and that Ray had too, but it wasn't enough and would never be enough, the act of allowing Kincaid to live as unforgivable as it should be. Spawning an empire and a subscriber list I'd hunt until my days upon this world were done. Moreover, I would end him the moment we found him again.

Presently, however, there was work to do, and as I walk to the man in blue flannel who gave up Kincaid's name, I raise the axe once more. Hands blocking his face, he recedes, cowers, bodies on either side of me falling as fast as the flesh covering their bones is ripped apart by gunfire. I continue. Down and through this man until the concrete beneath his body begins to spark. I separate him. Quarter him. And before we burn everything to the ground, I come to understand two things at once: I wouldn't hear right for a week, longer possibly, and experience, like I said earlier, it's more than a teacher.

For some, it's a way of life.

POLISH AND SHINE

I knew this guy once. Bender was his name. Burly dude who worked in the meat department at a grocery store. Cut meat, packaged hamburg. Stuff like that. You remind me of this guy, Neal, right down to that receding hairline. Hey, eyes up here, princess.

So Bender's story, like your story, it's a human-interest story, and really, is there any other kind? It's a story that involves you, Neal, but not upfront-like. Much like me, much like Bender himself, you are a side character in this tale, but since we both know you're a back-door type of individual, I think you may know where this is headed. What? Oh, I see. Wasn't my intention, Neal, but seriously, you really have no one to blame but yourself

Ah, don't give that look, Neal. We barely know one another. Well, that's not entirely true now, is it? Back door or not, we both know you're the type of person this world could use a whole lot less of.

Anyway, I've gotten ahead of myself—again.

So, a while back we catch wind of an enterprise that should not exist. I'm talking human trafficking here, Neal, but something tells me you already know this too. We catch wind, as I said. We put out lines. One asshole leads to another asshole and then in a basement much like this warehouse, a man mentions a bar just before he's relieved of his head.

There's that word again. Yes, Neal, I *can* see how it looks like I may be doing such a thing on purpose. I'm not, of course, not really, but then again, what if I am?

Anyway, a man named Bishop Rider is responsible for most of this. A man who—

Yes, I see my mistake now. Doesn't mean we're buds or anything, Neal. I just want you to appreciate how this all came to be. Not your part, Neal—no, you're a dirtbag. I just want to make sure you understand how things can, in fact, be seen through another person's eyes.

Bishop Rider, the man in question, he had a family once. This family is taken from him, however, and Neal, this happens in the unprettiest of ways. I'm talking men in masks, bodies in dumpsters, with rape and death forming the collision that brings us to today. Makes this man dedicate his life to a certain ritual is what it does. Laser focusing him, in other words. You see what it is I'm saying here, Neal?

Good. But wait, there's more!

It's not just the ring leaders, Neal. Nah, Rider is an equal-opportunity kind of guy. He goes after middlemen, starts side quests, people who may or may not own construction sites and build extensions out from the basements of pre-existing buildings.

Wait. *You* own a construction site? Neal, what *are* the fucking odds?

Hey, again, eyes up top, princess. Today is Neal day, let's not forget that.

So, Anthony Kincaid. He rings some bells for you as well, I bet. Oh, shake your head all you want, Neal, but yeah, Seeley Construction—we already know. You think you'd be in that concrete if we didn't. Neal, dude, please, a little bit of credit.

And I want to say you didn't know what you were contracted to build in the basement of that bar, but no, Neal, I can't. *We* can't. It doesn't jive. It don't fly. It fails to do anything but put you in that ground the same way it has so many others.

What? You think this warehouse doesn't have history? Neal, you need to get some new expressions. Those tears and that mewling will only take you so far. But here, let me give you a tour.

This place, it's privately owned. You trace it hard enough it goes back to Rider via an associate, sure, but that's neither here nor there. I *have* been watching you eyeball those machines, though. Yessir, I have. You have a few of them yourself, if I'm not mistaken. The cement mixer, that's a special grade, brought in proper a couple years ago. I told you this place has history, Neal.

Like this spot here, the one I'm standing on. Man by the name of John Foster occupies the space beneath. And over here, this spot here, is a man named Vincent Marshall. Four steps to my right and we have Eugene Cusie. Behind him and past those skids on the right lie Rachel Derman and Kimberly Basso, and beside those fuckin' peaches rests our old pal Bender. You remember Bender, Neal? He of the packaged hamburg and cut meat? Yeah, of course you do.

Fucking evil pieces of shit, every fucking one of them. But be prepared, Neal, as what's about to go down, it's going last. Not last last. I mean, I'm not going to wait around for you to starve. Nothing like that. It means this place is full of adventure neither of us can see. I'm talking rodents, Neal, in case you're having trouble carrying the one. Years ago, Rider used a bunch of them when trying to teach a man much like you the lesson *he* required.

Did it take? Hell no, and the man went out smelling like peanut butter if you must know. Why peanut butter? You're a smart-enough shitbird, Neal, I'm sure you can figure that one out.

Last thing before we get to it, then. I'm on my own tonight. Most times I'm just what you'd call the pre-game, but the big guy, him and some other like-minded individuals, they got a line on the very man who connects us tonight. Some might call that irony, Neal. Others, coincidence. Who knows, though. What I do know, Neal, is this: it means you and me, we are mano-a-mano for the duration. Well, not really. As all you're going to do is huff behind that gag as I spread this jar of Jif over the only part of your body our friends in the corners can see. They're going to take you down to the bone too, Neal, just so you know. I'm not sure if your eyes will go last or not, either, but I'm thinking it's a pretty safe bet. Post eyeballs, however, it becomes a whole new ball game. First, I'll remove what's left. That's where the "masher" comes in. Technical term is steamroller, yes, but I've always felt masher gets the point across far better than roller. When that's done, it's time to say hello to my little friend! What, you never seen Scarface, Neal? Are you for real? Fine. Whatever.

Industrial sander, Neal. That's what happens next. The nub the top of your spine turns into becoming an off-colour mark upon this concrete and nothing more. Polish and shine, baby! Polish and shine.

What? You think it's too much? Over the top? Yeah, that's fair. Or close enough to fair. Either way, it's going to happen, Neal, so elaborate or not, does it really fucking matter?

Of course it does!

Neal. Neal, Neal, Neal.

I thought you were listening this whole time. Neal: people like you only understand things one of two ways.

You're here to experience both.

SHAUN BARLOW STAPLES

Around the same time Jeramiah and I are teaching Levinson Ducard how to fly, Shaun Barlow Staples is working hard at hiding the man he truly was.

Long, dark hair preceding him, the papers presented him as the guy next door, an owner of a chain of grocery stores, and from what would be found out only after he's dead, harbored a love of horror films like no other.

All shit, of course. If you're a monster, you're a monster—a truth I have lived with for the better part of thirty years. That you maintain the dexterity to fool enough people and live amongst them undetected, that's just an upgrade not many can conceive of—born of necessity or otherwise.

And no one wants to be caught, not of the majority, but sometimes people go above and beyond, and that elevation, if radared by someone like me, it means all bets aren't just off but that I would ensure some type of poetry made it into the proceedings to come if an opportunity went and presented itself.

Not always, no, but more frequent as time has gone on. These pieces of shit deserving of so much more than the death they would experience, and me, a man more than willing to travel those extra three miles. Be it by axe, by hammer or, situation permitting, adapting the same type of method some of them had been using for years.

Come sundown, Shaun Barlow Staples would understand this all too well. Oh yes, in-fucking-deed.

* * *

"How in the absolute fuck does this guy make bail?" It's a valid question, but I don't care and tell Jeramiah as much. What's the point? Staples was out; he had become available. And really, that was all that mattered.

"Think of it like a birthday. You and me, we're about to open a present." A comedian I was not, but Jeramiah flashes me a smile all the same. Same smile as his father. Same slicked back hair too, while I'm at it. But that's where any similarity between the two men ceased to be. Some bone structure remained, sure, but the human components Jeramiah's father lacked, they stood tall in the man sitting opposite me. And even though I lump myself in with people like Jeramiah's father, I know I work differently, a reaction to an action, let's say, and more than anything, I'm only a reflection of the men I hunt. My methods, however, they are no less lethal than the madness I'm attempting to destroy.

"You have a lead, I take it?"

Of course I did. I wouldn't have called him otherwise. "Staples believes he has the ability to get away with things. It means Staples has been spotted out and about. Care to take a ride?"

He looks at me, there from his side of the booth. "Ray?"

I wipe my hands with a napkin, "Ray's been keeping an eye, yes. Staples going on with his life like grocery items are the only things he's ever sold."

Jeramiah smiles again. "This asshole is going to wish he stayed locked up, isn't he? Fuck, I can just tell."

I don't answer. I finish my beer and drop forty to the table instead. Jeramiah follows suit.

Outside, toward the van, my silence continues. But it's not because of Jeramiah. I am what I've become. I cannot deny that fact. Men like Staples, I see myself in them. Fair or unfair, it remains a truth I've known for years. Tonight, a man would die. He would beg as well, and I'd like to say the dying part was the ultimate goal, and it is, but I'd be lying if I said I wasn't looking forward to the inevitable. No, not once I've found out what they've done.

It's late but warm, and Ray is coming out of the Buchannon place as we pull up. Perched high and looking down upon Culver as it did, it has been my second home since before I knew Jeramiah existed and just after his father killed the only family I had. "I modified the hydraulics—tweaked them, anyway. Strong as you two are, each of you on either side of him should do the trick." Trick or not, I no longer questioned when Ray got to tinkering. The man could build, and like me, was battling the darkness of this world the only way he knew how. "Man has a lot of inclinations toward mistaken identity too," he continues. "He's backing this up with people are out to get him, so yeah, there's that." He smiles as he says this, of course, but then shrugs and turns to leave.

"You're not joining us?"

"Kid, having the three of us down there is only going to crowd the occasion," he says. "You and Bishop, you got this. Besides, there's still that Kolakowski fella to be looked into. Think it might be better if I start in on that."

Did I or Jeramiah argue? No, I can't say that we did.

Not when there was work to be done.

Batista and I once tracked a man who owned an appliance store. In the basement of this store was a room that should not have existed. A room full of monitors and screens depicting things recorded and images that were live. Before this room, however, lay another room. A workroom. Better yet, a worktable, one that held vises on either side of the front of it. We placed this man's hands into these vises, popping his fingertips like grapes.

It's not how this man ends, no, but it is how his ending begins.

The construct Shaun Barlow Staples found himself within was a larger version of those vises. And Christ, it wasn't even Christmas.

Shirtless, the thick hair of his upper body lay drenched in sweat from his continued attempts at escape. He could not remove himself, of course, as his ankles were chained to the floor while his wrists sat tethered to the tops of the metal that made up each side of the vise. Standing, he was sandwiched erect from just below his breasts to the top of his hips.

Jeramiah removed his gag.

"Any price. *Any* price. You name it, it's fucking yours." He sucks at the air, taking it in through both his mouth and nose. His eyes remained focused, however, buggy but never leaving mine. "It's always money with men like you, Shaun," I say and look to the surgical table to my left. Turning back, I continue, "People who feel they're able to buy their way out of just about anything. And that just, please do take it as being emphasized." I'd like to say this wasn't how the world worked, but Staples being before us as he was, it proved me wrong as it had hundreds of times before. Granted, a five million retainer or bond *was* the highest I'd ever seen, but still.

"Your families, then. I'll make it generational. I will make it so your grandchildren's grandchildren will never have to work a day in their lives."

"And what about the lives you've already ruined?" He looks toward Jeramiah, but where I thought defeat would come into the man's stubbled face, none does.

"You want me to say I'm a monster? We're all fucking monsters. You think you're any fucking different? This here, me here like this, what the fuck does that make you?"

"Not you." And the silence, it takes hold of this man in ways I've rarely seen. The only sound for the next five seconds coming from the fluorescents above.

"Names, then. I can give you names. You think I do this shit myself?" At one time, maybe, but once Ray went digging and found what he did, I no longer could. Staples doesn't need this information, not really, but as he continues, it happens. The names he speaks linking to a chain of dirtbags we'd already dealt with—one I hadn't thought about in years. What surprises me, though, is how these Armenians never once crossed my mind. We get lucky later, sure, through a man named Burke, but here at this point in time, I should have caught the connect. Involving cribs, infants, and a dirty sergeant named O'Bannon, you'd think every one of their names would be burned into what passes for my soul.

And yet...

"Well?" He's not quite indignant but something along that line rings true. Privilege, perhaps. Either way, it unleashes the final push and as each of us takes a side, Staples' head becomes a swivel, unable to choose who to concentrate upon.

We do not go slow. We do not go fast. We only turn until his words devolve into screams and bones relent to pressure. Unyielding, his midsection remains intact, but as syrup-like blood spills from his mouth and coats his chin, his straining subsides, and a thick gurgling begins. We continue undaunted, however, the built-in hydraulics assisting our respective cranks until he erupts, effectively halved, and organs that once helped this man traffic humans could no longer go by the names they once were.

Dripping, covered in gore, I look across to Jeramiah. Through a mask of red, he smiles.

For the first time in maybe forever, I do the same.

PROSPECTION

On paper, Ethan Jennings presented exactly as stated. Five eleven, blue eyes, blonde hair, and far from the dental hygienist/amoral piece of human garbage he actually was. He'd hid himself well in other areas too, his social media accounts as clean as they came and beyond reproach. Isn't until we dig into the man's downloads that we find the smoking gun we were looking for.

"It's a swap show, more or less. No actual intel if any of them have gone further, but these videos, Bishop, fuck these videos, they're reason enough for me." There's an edge to his voice, and his jaw clenches in a way that wasn't new. And I'm not saying Jeramiah and I were exactly alike, but then again, you'd never catch me arguing the point. One step better, and these dirt-bags, men like Jennings, they tend to graduate from thought to deed and by the time this occurs, as Jeramiah suggested, it's too late. Not always, no, but I like to keep things simple when I can.

"We do them together," I say to Jeramiah. "Be nice for them to see what it's like to experience things from the other end."

"The man with the plan." But the edge in his voice remained, and from the back end of a full parking lot, we watch as Jennings exits his place of employment, him and a couple of his co-workers huddling together before going their separate ways. It's overcast, the sky a bruise, but the man's teeth are what I'm concentrating on. Large, straight, and white, I picture them as they needed to become: broken, removed, and attached to bits of flesh that come along for the ride.

I exit the van.

I've said this before, but it bears repeating—Jeramiah has always been the money. Better still: I couldn't have done half the things I've done without him. This isn't to say Batista, Ray, and I didn't get on before he came into our lives. I'm only saying he made portions of it easier. Not all, but a greater amount since John retired. What Batista provided, fighting the outcome or not, we'd never get back, that was a given. His access to informants, parole dates, and last-minute tips to outgoing warrants disappearing the moment he turned in his badge. Jeramiah proved a different channel than Batista is all, at times taking longer to get what we required, sure, but once we had it, once we did, the dividends it paid outweighed my patience at a margin of ten to one.

It's how Jennings popped into view—involving trigger words and virtual land mines set up over a decade ago, all of it linking to a certain subscriber list.

Kincaid.

Dying under the heel of my prosthetic, his skull more mush than bone by the time I was done, the man was years in the past. But like the Navarro/Grimes recordings, Kincaid's dealings upon this earth remained a gift that wasn't really a gift at all.

"Control is what this is about, Ethan. Arrogance, too, I suppose. I mean, ten years after the fact and you chose to not only download what you did but send it to Frick and Frack here." Frick and Frack were Bill Hostetter and Jensen Frill, both bound, seated, and facing Jennings. Bigger than the man beside him, Hostetter had thin, unwashed hair and an overbite that took in most of his gag. Frill, an endomorph, wore a wifebeater, jeans, and a puddle that continued to drink at the crotch of those jeans.

Ethan Jennings, on the other hand, was shirtless, vertical, and strapped to an inversion table. The gash above his right eye, the one he received before I got him in the van, now a clotted, angry mess.

"I'll make you a deal," I say, addressing Hostetter and Frill. "First man who doesn't look away gets to keep his head." Jeramiah steps forward, mini chainsaw gripped in his left hand. Both men look to him. Both men then proceed to lose color, and in Frill's case, a little more liquid south of the border.

"You may not have fully acted upon the impulses you have, but the child in those videos, she was four. Each of you chose to watch it. Each of you sought it out. There is no one here to blame but yourselves."

Their muffled pleas start in unison, but Jennings is who I concentrate on. And what comes out of his mouth as I remove his gag is what always comes out of their mouths once we entered this part of the equation. I don't answer, though, not how you think. I invert the table back to level instead and start in on his teeth as I knew I would. Removed, I pull him back up, his mouth a swollen, receding mess. Hostetter and Frill, however— they remained faithful throughout and don't look away until I start in with the bone saw.

Jeramiah moves forward, bringing his machine to life as I start mine. Hostetter becomes shorter for his own trouble, and me, I take the bottom part of Jennings's jaw. The man goes limp through the process, sure, but losing him to shock or not, his tongue hangs like a tie by the time I pull the last piece of bone free.

I turn to Frill.

"You only watched; you didn't participate. That's how you're trying to reconcile it. It's how men like you operate. But it's more than reconciliation, and it always will be. It's the opposite and culpability rolled into one. Today is your day to learn."

Would he? Did it even matter?

Thirty years on, the answer remained what it had to be. What it needed to be. I move forward, determined to make him understand.

* * *

And understand he does. So much so that near his end, down both ears and a thumb, he gives me a name where I thought no name could be found. In turn, it leads me to believe we'd been wrong about the man. That he'd perhaps been into things deeper than first imagined. Either way, it produces a name Frill screams repeatedly as Jeramiah changes course and starts taking parts of his forearm away in strips. It nets us a house, but in between hurried, chaotic breaths, Frill says something else, a string of words, and ones I hadn't heard in years.

"Address please," Jeramiah says, and Frill, head lolling, spits out the street and number like his life depended on it.

Upstairs, Jeramiah boots up his favorite screen and looks to verify. Match complete, we head back to Frill and his new sense of urgency once he realizes it's an incinerator he's being steered toward. We follow this up with Hostetter, Hostetter's head, and Jennings as the man begins to rouse. Jeramiah under his one shoulder and me under the other, blood spray and bits of enamel sputter loose as he attempts to speak. It's gibberish, of course, but I give the man marks for trying. Hard as his hands cling over the sides of the incinerator's neck, however, he can only hold onto the metal for so long. The gibberish morphing into a warbling cry once gravity and exhaustion push him past his breaking point.

It left cleanup, and as I grab the wall hose, I think back to what I mentioned earlier, in regard to life pre-Jeramiah. His money made things easier, yes, and if one looked hard enough, sure, there was some poetry to be found in the situation as well. His father's death, perpetrated by Batista and yours truly, becoming the catalyst that activated the insurance policy bankrolling what I have yet to turn from. But even so, it couldn't last forever, and like most things, you either accepted the fact or did something about it. This was my war, not Jeramiah's. And even though I could see him carrying on without me, I'd never ask it

of him. Besides, I'd never know. Not for sure.
But what I can tell you is this: a man could dream.

ROOM 16

A lifetime ago there'd been a list. It involved a dirty cop and his informant, and it worked far better than I'd hoped. Leaving this world not only a better place in the process but one that allowed me for a little while to believe in the things I no longer could. Some saw the error of their ways by the end of these discussions. Others, not so much. Could I blame them? I did and still do.

The names upon that list lighting me up in such a way that a type of rashness began to take hold, one that I try my best to keep in check, even here, as I find myself near the end.

"A rocket launcher, really?" Batista says, and in that moment, I knew exactly where the conversation was headed. "You have any spare tanks I should know about then?" I took his point. How could I not? If I wanted to keep doing what needed to be done, I had to be more selective in how I chose to go about things.

I had to be precise.

It led to the Buchannan house becoming a sort of home away from home in the intervening years. Not always, no, but enough of my time was being spent there that Ray takes it upon himself to upgrade the facility, a certain basement in particular.

I wouldn't change how this occurred either, not even after Ray and Batista complete their watch. The methods by which both men go out, however, this I would change. It's a nice dream, sure, but my inner pragmatist and make-believe have never quite seen eye to eye.

Brings us back to the here and now—back to a face that

looked back at me from the laptop Jeramiah had turned my way. "Look familiar?" It didn't. Not the excess chins or the indented scars above the man's right eye. But the name that accompanied the image, this I did recall.

"You've been keeping tabs?" We are, in fact, at the aforementioned Buchannan house, but upstairs, in the civilized part of the building. Jeramiah pushes back from the table and folds his arms. In jeans and a white T-shirt, he's the same as he's ever been. His hair may be a little thinner, a little greyer, but it would never dull the man inside. "I was taught by the best, Bishop. The big man would expect nothing less." Batista. John. Gone now, of course, but never forgotten. And a man whose words I think of still.

Was a time the detective kept tabs for me too, his position within the CCPD his means to our end. Jeramiah, though, he used the money his father's death left him in this regard. The kicker there being it was the detective and I who'd removed Marcel Abrum from the board in the first place, making what was to be our future far more manageable in the process. Resource-wise, I mean. And sure, it may have involved a wheelbarrow and the stacking of body parts no longer connected to the whole, but when I choose to look back on this particular time in my life, it fails to feel like the history it is, but rather, something that was meant to be. If I'm honest, becoming an outcome I required.

But the boy Jeramiah had been, he becomes a man who eventually seeks me out, and to this day continues to use those resources as he had back at the start.

Case in point: the here and now.

The man looking back at me from the laptop. Mike Friesen. A man whose name was written upon a list created lifetimes ago. A man who'd been serving time when this all went down. A man who could finally pay.

Time to finish the work.

* * *

Hospice on the Hill did in fact live up to the branding. It sat below the Rob Smith Memorial bridge as well, and as I exited the van, its shadow loomed large.

Two blocks from my intended target, this part of Culver thrived, the streets teeming with life and devoid of a type of filth home to a different part of Culver.

But for Friesen to end up here of all places meant money was somehow in play. Money or favours owed. Men like Friesen, they don't get released from a sentence such as his only to have it swapped for a facility that specialized in what it did. All told, it meant a little more digging might yet come into play.

Little black bag in hand, I transfer my cane to the same hand and open one of the wooden double doors. There are claw foot benches on each side of these doors, empty but for a purple walker, silver chimes hanging from the handles.

"Relative or friend?" I look to my left, toward a man whose name tag read Felix. Bearded and clothed in white from head to shoe, he reminds me of Batista. Not Batista as he would come to be, however, but from a time when the detective was in his prime. A tad shorter, perhaps, but no less thick.

I answer as I knew I would—cousin—and same as I had in so many others, jot a false signature in the sign-in book displayed before me. Was a time I would be scrutinized a little more than I was, but age, more so the cane, brought forth advantages I couldn't deny.

"Elevator is to the left." I nod and walk on, my head at the angle it needed to be. It's here the smell envelopes me. Thick and cloying, it's everywhere at once, and try as I might, I could no longer see this as a future I would escape. I'd try, sure, but in the end, we all succumb, wanted or otherwise. Granted, this *was* my first hospice, but still, the realist in me remained.

I move on, pass a theater/rectory room and then beyond the elevator I was never going to take. The hallway is wide, plush carpeted, the crème-coloured walls punctuated with landscapes and bodies of water every six feet or so. Encompassing all this and as cloying as the smell is a feeling, an atmosphere, and one as solemn as it should be. The end stages of the life lived here, full of cocktails created to counteract the agony your body puts you through once it begins to dine upon itself full-time. It again reminds me of what my own remaining days promised, but then, as ever, I remember why I'm here.

I turn right, then right again, and along this corridor, a care worker—red hair, mid-forties, slim—asks if I need assistance. No, I tell her, but if I did, I'd be sure to ask. Beyond me, I turn back and watch as she goes. Turning the corner, sure she is gone, I step to door 16.

And enter the fray.

The smell within is the same, but it's also different. Darker somehow. Thicker. A small hallway leads to an open room on my left that held a bed placed between two slim wall units. Upon this bed, hooked to IV lines tethered to these cabinets lay Friesen, uncovered, unconscious, and wearing light blue pajamas.

I turn back and from my pocket produce a wedge to secure the door. Done, I stand over Friesen, removing the call button from his reach. He's thinner now, a good hundred pounds below his mug shot from back in the day. The scars remain though, deep and above his right eye.

A gag and tape come next, and his eyes do open as I lift his head to wrap it around, but they fail to register the significance of what's being done to him. Head back down on his pillow, it begins.

"You don't get off that easy, Mike. Not after everything you've done. And I know you think you've known pain, that this here is the be-all/end-all to everything you've ever gone through. Believe me when I say what I have planned will fail to compare by the time we part ways." I'm right; he doesn't understand. Not how I want. And I'd like to take credit for what happens next, but no, I can't, Jeramiah being the one who brought it up and modified the very contents of the syringe I inject in the IV drip to my right.

Doesn't take long after that—someone's eyes as big as Os in the span of seconds.

"Counter agent," I tell him and tap the man's sunken chest with one gloved hand as I do. "It's a good thing too, Mike. Gets us so we're on the same page as it has. It also means what happens next, it becomes everything it should be. Everything it needs to be."

I go on, of course, and inform him of the list and how his name came to be on it and then of the men who created it. I tell him the order of things as well, of how most of it went down, ending my trip down memory lane with a man named Garth and how from the top of an abandoned silo this man came to eat concrete in the way every depraved individual should. Did Friesen understand all this? Of course he did. They always do.

"But you remained out of reach, Mike. Untouchable. If I'm honest, it's more than likely the reason you were forgotten about." True. But I forgo Jeramiah's part and how he'd chosen to keep tabs. I could have informed Friesen of this particular event, sure, but no, I'd already been here longer than I planned.

It meant time, she was a wasting.

And only after turning on the wall-mounted TV and raising the volume to an acceptable level do I remove the tin snips from my bag.

There is pushback to this, and panic. Friesen, more so his head, trying its best to merge with his pillow in a way I'd witnessed before. His hands come up too, simultaneously, onto the rails of his bed, but he's too weak, his wrists more bone than skin.

I move to the foot of the bed.

Weak, his protests continue, his muffled mewling intensifying the moment he feels the metal touch his skin. Was a time I could take all five digits at a go, but alas, even though my mind remained game, my body was far less cooperative.

I redouble my efforts, add leverage, and with a familiar release, the big toe finally drops free. Process repeated, I improve the count by five, and then I double it, adding two more to the pile once I've reached his eyes. It's here the shock sets in, however— the remaining parts of those eyes more sludge than iris by the time he shuts down, each one slow and sliding through the hollows of his face as it worked toward the chin.

I could have spoken here. I'd planned to. I don't, though. I only finish what needed to be done. Move to open the man's bed shirt and upon his chest write something I hadn't in years: FOLLOW THE CHILDREN. A blast from the past, yes, but I was in the endgame now, and if a decades-old list could somehow bear fruit in the here and now, then maybe, just maybe, an old standby could too.

Either way, it would have to do.

Either way, I finished the work.

BIG BUSINESS BREAKING SMALL CUNTS

Jeramiah is nine when I kill his uncle and father. Fifteen when I do his grandfather. It connected us as you'd think, but similar as our paths become, they're just as divergent. In my world, I envision revenge, vengeance, or a variation of the two to punctuate our eventual union. In Jeramiah's, the opposite occurs, and flipping it, he chooses redemption over retribution. In name only, of course, and long before I even knew he existed.

"His cruelty is what I remember most. The way he treated my mother, the yelling and the sunglasses she always wore once the yelling stopped." It wasn't often he brought his father up, wasn't often I did either, but sometimes the demons that shape us, they become the thing that drives us too.

Big business breaking small cunts.

I've only heard two men say these words. The first was Marcel Abrum, Jeramiah's father, the man doing so before he unloads a shotgun into my chest. The Kevlar saves me, yes, but the words remain. The second man was Kincaid, courting suicide and on a table before I'm back removing parts of his limbs. However, it's when a different man repeats these words that I don't only become interested, but full-on committed.

Frill, the man in question, he comes to us via a dental hygienist named Jennings. A piece of shit if there ever were, and one who too ends up being down body parts by the time we end the night's festivities. But Frill, once we're through with Jennings and his buddy, he sings the song, dances the dance, all in an attempt to save what he should had known was already over. Name and address verified, it ushered in the cleanup portion of the evening, and headfirst we introduce Frill to his final resting place, protesting screams and all.

But his words remained, a phrase I hadn't heard in years, and though I didn't yet know it, it would merge the present with the past in ways I couldn't fully predict.

No, not fully.

Bruce Monroe was the name Frill gives up, and after some digging, he proves to be a man partial to the resources money can bring: all purchases, legit or otherwise, done online, by phone, and delivered through a gate to a "house" that overlooked the eastern tip of Culver Bay. The bluffs incorporated into the structural design of not only his house but that of his four neighbors, topping out at over six figures apiece—sleek, modern, and affixed with as many right angles as panes of glass.

Bruce Monroe, less so.

His years of reclusion softening him in ways the pictures we had on file failed to capture. Grey hair slick and unwashed, he dozed in a beige recliner, his ankles swollen and his yellow toenails curled and like bone. Behind him, ceiling-high glass stretched from the kitchen and beyond the room we now stood, the night looking back in and toward us, dark as a mouth. A wall-mounted 80-inch TV sat to his left, bracketed by shelves of DVDs, VHS tapes, and yes, some vinyl. To his right, a writing desk upon which stood an open laptop. Further down, below a collection of Rockwell paintings and electric wall sconces set to low, beckoned a leather couch, but one in front of even more glass, the coffee table itself sitting higher than most.

I sit. Clear my throat. And observe Monroe as he rises from unconsciousness. He's silent, which was a different way to go, sure, and continues to regard me as he adjusts his La-Z Boy to its original position. There was a dent in his forehead, one I hadn't noticed, and I watch as gravity gives life to pre-flattened jowls.

"How did you get in here?"

"Same way I'll get out." For truth, it was Jeramiah, but Monroe, he didn't need to know that.

"I could scream,"

"You could," I agree, but he doesn't. He picks at the arms of his leather chair instead. It was a game, of course, and one only the guilty choose to play.

"Are you here to kill me?" Ah, paydirt. We begin.

"Depends," I say and sit forward on the couch. "On what, well, that's up to you too. Let's say we start with the room downstairs." Tucked in a corner beside an unused garage, it held a small cot and a door home to too many scratches.

"I don't...I don't do that anymore. I haven't for years." He's sweating now, and his hand animations cause his robe to open, exposing dense grey hair.

"Even if I believed you, you think that changes things?" Jeramiah takes his cue, and from behind a suddenly startled Monroe, he moves past the man, black duffel bag in hand. He sets the bag on the ground beside the coffee table, hunkers down, and removes the mini chainsaw. A handheld blowtorch follows, accompanied by two ball peen hammers, a funnel, and three Red Delicious apples. The fruit? Yeah, your guess is as good as mine.

"Wait...you don't have to do this. I told you..."

"But Bruce, here's where you're wrong. The statute of limitations on being a dirtbag, there are none. The things you've done, they can't be absolved."

It changes then, and what I'd only suspected, I now knew for certain. The widening of his eyes was only a bonus. Enlarging in a way I have only seen a few times in life—when they come to realize they know exactly who I am.

"You're him," he says. "You're the guy." I hold my hand up to Jeramiah as I see it dawn on his face. Should I have told him beforehand? Perhaps. But I wanted to be sure.

"I am, Bruce. But what many fail to realize is this: I had help that night." True. But back then, and unlike now, Batista and I used hatchets to cut up Jeramiah's father. "But what I'd really like to discuss is the reason you became a recluse. I'm smart enough to figure it out myself, but you, Bruce, I think it best if you address the class."

He wouldn't, though. His chest suddenly the most important thing in the world. Fine, we'd do it the long way then.

"And Bruce, if I'm off here, please, correct me." And when I mention Miranda Abrum, I have to still Jeramiah once more. His frustration is understandable, warranted even, but closure in the lives of people like us, it didn't happen often. Again, I wanted to be sure.

"Big business breaking small cunts. Where had I heard that before—that's what started this, Bruce. Your boy Frill, he mentions it as Jeramiah is ripping him apart. It gets me thinking, Bruce, about how unique a phrase it actually is, and how I'd only ever heard two people speak it aloud."

"I worked for Abrum, so what?" And there was some spine to his reply. Good. We could end this proper yet.

"It means some of the people involved that night, Abrum's death overshadowed what they'd been doing before I intervened. Odonnavitch we found a few years ago, but the others, they never give up who cut Jeramiah's mother into pieces."

Jeramiah looks at me. "Wait. What?"

I tell him my suspicions. The wheelbarrow. His mother's remains. That even though it had been his father who ordered it, it was the man in front of us who saw to the deed.

Jeramiah moves forward.

And Bruce, like a pro, he reads the room. "It wasn't me. Christ, I'm telling ya, it wasn't fuckin' me!"

I begged to differ, stating it *was* him, even if he failed to lift a finger. "You were part of Abrum's circle. It was asked of one of you. It was carried out by one of you. You aren't innocent. You never were." And as Batista and I did to Jeramiah's father, so to do Jeramiah and I do to Monroe. Starting with the man's legs at his knees, his arms at the elbow, and stacking the appendages that come into his lap like wood. I cauterize, of course, but the gore we produce is immense, and the man's heart gives out by the end.

"Did you know?" I don't lie. But I don't tell him the whole truth either.

"I had a hunch," I offer, and start the van. "But understand, Jeramiah, I wanted to be sure." It was enough, and perhaps better than I would have reacted had the roles been reversed, he nods his approval.

Did it change things? If it did, he never tells me, but then again, I didn't expect him to. Keeping it from him for the short time I did had been the right choice, the pragmatic choice, and thrust upon him or not, it gave me the opportunity to do something I never thought I'd be able to. What he, Batista, and Ray had already done for me.

I ensured he could grieve.

FUCK HOUSES

Things change once you separate a man from his appendages. There's no denying this. Like time itself, it's as constant as it is immutable. And as that perfect understanding flickers to life that nanosecond before this separation occurs, a new level of belief is not only achieved but steps forward, screaming, to where those who find themselves on the receiving end of what I am finally realize that yes, I had meant every damn word I said in the moments prior.

Butkowski bleeds, screams, every vein upon his throat up and leading the choir. It's normal, of course, and Ray lets it play out a beat or two longer than I might have.

"It's not much, Butkowski," he says. "But rest assured, I won't be offering twice." The towel hits Butkowski square in the face, his huffing and chugging for a second obscured as the material clings to his beard. To his credit, the man reacts faster than most, the towel up against where it should be as I reach down for the part of him that lay on the floor. Not yet cold, I place it on the kitchen table in front of him and beside the remnants of the rope we'd used to hold his arms against the wood. Blood is most everywhere now. The expansive button-down he'd greeted us in far from the white it used to be. His chin and face and fridge to the right as peppered in splatter as the windows behind me. Points for distance there, of course. Oh yes, indeed.

"Now that we fully understand one another, I'm going to ask you the same question." He looks up from the blooming towel, his good eye both in shock and filled with that fear of understanding I mentioned. In a perfect world, this would happen before any type of reduction occurred. Inside that perfect world, however, men like me wouldn't need to do the things I've done. "Your answer checks out, Ray here ends things quick. You lie, prolong the inevitable, or anything along those types of lines, we're going to take that other hand." To accentuate the point, Ray pulls the blowtorch from his bag and sets it in the middle of the table.

One beat. Two.

"Fine," he says, and though the resentment is palpable, it comes as no surprise. "I'm a dead man either way. You or him, it's all the fucking same." Maybe. Maybe not. But as he says what he does I admit to not fully comprehending how my life and who he'd been working with would come to create the change it does. Not in the exact moment anyway. But the train I'd been placed upon, it had picked up speed—using the type of momentum it would require to catch me off guard.

And sure, looking back as I am, it's easy to say I should have known. That I should have seen. That Alex had been MIA for weeks. But really, that type of disappearance from Alex, it wasn't so far from the norm. Still, hindsight can only take a person so far. And betrayal, it's never done in plain sight.

It meant sooner rather than later Butkowski and I would come to have at least one more thing in common.

I'd bounce back, of course. Butkowski, however, would not.

Mapone.

Not my worst mistake, no, but up there. A nasty piece of meat with a voice that ran counter to how you thought it should, I'd effectively neutered him in front of a different fuck house. On its front lawn to be precise and using a spoon to remove his last working eye. Again, the message this would send—this was the goal.

Wrong. So very fucking wrong.

A collision course had to occur as well, after the fact, and this is where Alex comes into play. His betrayal, him seeking out Mapone, the reason me and treadmills no longer see eye to eye. But here now, back before they track me to Buchannan and knock me out from behind, we had *this* fuck house to deal with.

City-bound, Batista had taken the girls from the premises hours ago. The big man intent on removing them as fast as we could. It left Butkowski, the information I hoped he held, and two other dirtbags zip-tied down below.

"And this house, it's the only one Mapone's been using? Again: Think wisely, Jay. There's more than what's already come out of that bag." Ray was far into it now. That hard little lean-in of his a pretty big tell. Not that I minded, of course. I'm only stating I was aware.

"We are it," Butkowski says, and I can see the color draining from his face in real time. Beads of sweat across his forehead rolling and mixing with the blood already there. "He wanted to…start small, under the radar. I think…you know why." And he almost smiles. But yeah, I did know why. I'd scared Mapone. Unfortunately, just not enough for him to remain the message I wanted him as.

"You promised if I told you, you'd make it quick. Maybe we start that process now?" Ray chuckles, but it's a humourless sound. More of a *can you believe this shit* response in nonverbal form. Me, I just get on with it, and moving forward, reach down into the bag.

I'm still surprised when they believe us, however. I really, truly am.

Full disclosure: we make it last.

We take him down to the joints and before he expires stack more of him than I thought we would. It isn't a prerequisite either, but stacking these pieces of shit, it's something that needs to be done. And good or bad, what I do has never been about saving people. No. It's about stopping them.

The kitchen is an abattoir too, slick from floor to ceiling fan and smelling of bodily fluids and whatever Butkowski had chosen for his last meal. The table drips. The chairs drip. Ray's handlebar mustache releasing its own droplets to the rhythm of his chest.

"Think I'm going to hit the van and change before we deal with the other two," he says, and the only clean flesh I'm able to see comes from where his goggles had been.

"Those other two," I say and drop my axe flat to the table. He stops, looks back, and I think he knew even before I spoke it aloud.

"Lemme guess, you have something else in mind?" Fingers guns comes next. His, not mine. But he wasn't wrong. Nope, not even close.

"Jack Storey." Ray holds the license he took from the man's back pocket further from his face. "I dunno, dude, I think you just can't grow a beard." Hogtied and muzzled, Storey grunts his response into the beige carpet, his gag an overflowing slick of spittle, snot, and sweat. He'd already pissed himself—a given, really, especially when you took into account how much Butkowski had screamed—but his bowels proved to be made of sterner stuff. His partner, however, a one Andy Rausch, he of the eyebrow rings and oversized jaw, had failed at keeping this same type of hold.

"I'll take his feet," I say. "You take the head." Done, we go back for Storey, and as we did to Rausch before him, ensure his head hits every door frame on the way out of the farmhouse.

Last, I call Batista and let him know Mapone was back in play. Then we light the place. The image in the van's rearview a bonfire writ large but receding as pavement stretches between us. Culver city lay due north. Hanson Falls behind us to the south. We drive, me behind the wheel, Ray in shotgun.

Our destination not twenty minutes away.

"Well, fuck me sideways. Look who the cat dragged in." Wearing dirty fatigues, he comes around the side of the barn as we're transferring Rausch from the van. The sun behind him, low and almost done for the day, one-armed Billy extends the only hand he can. "And hell, you two even brought friends."

He'd always had a way with words—*if they act like animals, maybe we should treat them like animals*—I'll give one-armed Billy that. As for personal hygiene, not so much. Not that I minded, as one-armed Billy was strictly part-time with regard to what I do. He was always up for helping out, of course, and I have always appreciated everything he gave.

"Could use a hand if you're offering, Bill," Ray says, and like that, it's on: the three of us in the barn with machetes in our hands and separating feet from shins and wrists from arms in under a minute and a half.

"Save the heads for last," Billy says, and as I watch him throw Storey's right thigh to his pigs, I step back and let him and Ray finish things.

Why? I can't say. Not in the moment. Now, however, is a completely different story.

I think I felt it coming. What Mapone was about to do. I couldn't have known, no, but as I said: things change once you separate a man from his appendages. It allowed me to weigh what occurred against everything it not only created but everything it allowed me to stop. One step beyond is Jeramiah, the influx of cash his addition brings, and then it's dirtbags like the Bone boys, the Gank brothers, and Jeramiah's father himself that enters my mind.

It's everything, that particular point in time. It takes from me, sure, but it also spurs me on. It also leads me to this, what I have come to acknowledge, embrace, and would say in less than forty-eight hours for the very first time.

For too long I'd been mistaking fate for coincidence.
I never would again.

BEHOLD, A PALE RIDER

The last time I'd thrown men from the rooftop of a building, wheelchairs had been involved. The men within those chairs as far from the God they'd chosen to hide behind. Consisting of afghans and liver spots, they were in appearance the exact opposite of the men now bound at my feet. Young or old, thick or thin, it wasn't their age that concerned me. What did was their bones and how we'd make them break.

"It's easy," I say, and almost touching, plant my cane in front of the middle one's nose. "And dirtbags like yourselves, tell me it hasn't crossed your minds. It means the first one of you to give up Pope is the first one who gets to leave."

It starts with Parks, the heavier one, his voice attempting to overtake his gag the only way it could. Like the arch of his back and the veins on his neck, it wasn't to be. Not how a man in his position would hope. Wifebeater and Tatts follow suit, of course, only to be outdone by Rondo, Pope's second in command. Ponytail down to his belt, wearing corduroy and plaid, he'd turned into what most of them do once they realize how close they'd come to their end. Priceless, in other words.

And me without my hat.

"I want to say they know something, Bishop. But, you know, I just don't think they do." Jeramiah steps through Rondo and Tatt-man as he says this. All three men upon their bellies and hogtied, the fine gravel and spreading dampness beneath Tatt-man a reaction that, for self-proclaimed "hard men," happened more than you'd think. It was just for show too, what Jeramiah says I mean, as no one but he and I would be leaving this rooftop alive, information given, taken, or otherwise.

As well, there'd been a sixth member to this morning's events, man by the name Tully, but Tully, big as he was, decided a stand was required and not ten minutes prior believed he was the one to take it. Jeramiah rebukes him, of course, and in the stairwell between the eighth and ninth floors puts a Bowie knife into the man's carotid in about the time it takes to blink. And yes, we *were* taking a chance doing things this way, but sometimes you come to realize that working from the shadows as we were, it can only take the message you're attempting to send so far. One step better and time steps up like it had never been, becoming the enemy you always knew it would.

Unfortunately, this was the end of the line. Of this particular stretch, I mean. Darkness being pulled into the light notwithstanding, I was too old to take things further. Had to trust the message we planned to send would do what was required, taking things in the direction I wanted them to go.

"It's possible," I say to Jeramiah, but I'm only biding our time, and I move toward the building's raised edge. Derelict, standing twelve storeys high, it was home to squatters at best and junkies at worst. Either way, it put us on the east side of Culver and directly upon Pope property. It meant decay surrounded us, this part of Culver much like a tooth in need of pulling. I've tried. Christ, have I. Some roots remain, however. Others, they refuse to die.

Jeramiah points. "You remember?"

Of course I did. The bridge beyond and above the fast-food joints, the abandoned factories, a place we'd once hung two men by chains. The chaser that night? A couple of fuck houses that never saw us coming. Ancient history, sure, and back to a time when chemo and I were not yet lovers, let alone adversaries who'd come to part ways. Did it change things? Not really. But it reminded me of what I couldn't escape: that my body would never be what it used to be and that it continued to eat at me from the inside.

"I do," I say, and watch as the buildings behind the bridge begin to reflect the morning sun. "I seem to remember what you did at those houses more. A good thing was done that night. Always better when everyone survives."

Jeramiah nods, the strengthening breeze and weeping behind us a reminder of why we'd chosen this place—that what we were about to do would reopen something that had been closed for years. Jeramiah turns, approaches Rondo and Tatt-man. He gets between them, squats, and then grabs them both by the binds on their wrists and lifts, bringing them back toward the bricked edge.

"Now you're just showing off," I say, and his smile is delayed somewhat, but it comes as he releases what he's carrying back to the ground. Only when he returns with Parks, the heavier one, does Jeramiah reply. "That's not showing off. *This* is showing off."

And I'd like to say Parks looked toward me as he flew by, but no, other things were occupying his mind. The concrete below for one, terminal velocity another. I could add the swing and subsequent arc Jeramiah implements as well, but again, I don't think it much mattered. What did was the look upon Rondo's upturned face and how Tatt-man was somehow receding into his.

I hunker down.

"And just so we're clear, none of you were leaving here the way you came. I wanted the light is all. Wanted you to see firsthand what men who choose to do the things you do will always deserve." True. All of it. But what I don't add is what I read as Jeramiah hoists Rondo by his wrists and neck and, like the man before him, jettisons him up and out until gravity is forced to take hold.

FOLLOW THE CHILDREN.

Landing a foot beyond from what remained of Parks, the

man's unleashed innards erupt and join the fray, the bone and blood of both men mixing and stretching toward the letters at an angle, the letters black, four feet high, and running the length of what had at one time been a community pool. Cracked and stained black in places, this pool no longer held water. Instead, it had become a collector of debris, garbage, and shopping carts rusted by years.

Jeramiah had added directional arrows as well, same size, same colour, pointing not only to the building we looked down from but through a vestibule littered with graffiti and broken glass. Past this, deeper, and along a certain hallway, you'd find yourself inside three refurbished apartments that shouldn't exist. But yet, here we were.

Was a time we never did this either. On the flipside, there'd also been a stretch we may have used the message Jeramiah wrote above the pool a little too much. We got lucky, however, and with Batista's help a decade ago shelved the very thing that almost brought us down. But here now, near the end of my time, I was done doing things how we had. Done working from the same shadows that protected the men we hunted. Tragedy, it has never defined me. Not how most would believe. If anything, it set parts of me free.

Hence FOLLOW THE CHILDREN and its revival. Hence our public display. And as I watch the last man sail past me, I know it's not the end. Close to it, sure, but I still had time. Batista remained topside, you see, and O'Bannon a gift not yet presented to me by Jeramiah himself. Add in the Hobin girl, those suitcases, and a certain 12-step circle-jerk I needed to see to believe, and it meant the work, it was far from over.

In a way, it'd just begun.

Case in point: Vernon Pope himself. And be it ego, pride, or a combination of the two, I will never not take the win, especially when it involves someone like Pope.

Big, brash, and in an eight-hundred-dollar suit, I never expected him to come out swinging like he does. Truth be told, I never expected to see the man at all; his money all the armor he required to shield himself from someone like me. But no, loud as he can, he rallies against the accusation we placed above that pool. And like a certain man who should have never been president, it works, muddying the waters, and I again watch a system I'd already turned my back on do what it has always done best.

But Pope, all six and a half raging feet of him, and despite the fake news gauntlet he'd thrown down, he at least remained a person of interest.

Was I disgusted with how it played out? That law enforcement could fumble a ball so completely as to let a man as guilty as Pope walk because he went at them as he did?

The answer, of course, is yes.

But throwing money at things or not, what it also did was open Pope to a different type of history.

My type of history.

"And I'll be honest," I say, and replace his glasses upon his face, making sure they sit as they should. I also watch as sweat runs from a carved forehead and down into a beard not long for this world. It meant he understood the situation. It meant, little round spectacles or not, he'd come to fully see. "I never thought things would end this way. If anything, I saw you ending up in a cell. If anything, I was content in knowing you'd rot your days away."

He tries to speak, but as it should, the gag holds back his lies. He tries to shift his body too, but no, the straps hold him as tight as they have so many others upon this table. It hadn't gotten much use of as late, not in the past couple of years, but then again, I should count myself lucky the Buchannan house remained at all.

"But men like yourself, you're unable to help yourself. Oh, you believe you can. Of that, I have no doubt. But men like me, Vernon, whether you refuse to accept it or not, I'm here because of men like you."

He's pleading now, his eyes and voice straining for the exact same shade of mercy people like him withhold without a thought. It's pathetic. It's just. It's everything he deserved and more.

Only when Jeramiah and what he carries is finally observed does this go up a level. When the inevitable is fully realized and the muscles due south lose every last bit of control.

I look to Jeramiah there in the archway. He looks to me. We'd heard it too many times before. More times than not, right in this very room, coming from one of the two tables Pope was restrained upon. It changed nothing, of course. It brought no one back. All it did was give sound to the time we spent doing the things that needed to be done.

"You had everything to do with what went on in those buildings, Vernon. You weren't an active participate, no, but then again, this is where men like you think you're safe. Wrong, Vernon. So fucking wrong."

And then it happens. Jeramiah steps fully into the room, his right hand and the machete within it down at his side. He's in a green hoodie now too, but like his jeans, it lay protected from the spillage to come—the see-through body suit he now wore one that each of us had put on before.

Up beside Pope, he lowers the table the man rests upon, brings it down as far as it can go. He then straddles the table, his back now to Pope. Bending, he releases the man's left leg from its binding, pulling it up and tight to his chest. Craning his head back round, he says, "This is going to hurt. I'm going to make sure you feel it all. You believe in God, now would be the time."

Seconds pass. Gazes remain. And Jeramiah, though he doesn't smile, not how I thought he might, he is the first to blink, turning back round and at a downward angle hacking into the man's upper thigh like he would a tree.

Blood arcs, pantsuit shreds, and only when Jeramiah hits

bone does he step over and go at things from the other side; where he not only ensures the man will never again run but exposes parts of Pope that until this very moment had never seen the light of day.

I'd hoped for Pope to stay with us for longer than he does—for the man to witness Jeramiah holding his separated leg by the ankle as I witness it, but no, he short circuits almost out of the gate. When the meat of his right shoulder is brought into the festivities, however, he does, in fact, rise up and join us for a spell. When his eyes become fire and the veins on his neck and forehead expand to what I take for capacity. But it was over, him reviving a bit there at the end or not—the femoral artery doing what it did best whenever circulation is removed from the equation.

And here too, it didn't change things, Pope bleeding out as he does. All told, it never would. Because no matter how much I wanted it, we'd never remove them all. I knew this. Jeramiah knew this. Each of us long ago coming to the conclusion in ways both straightforward and unfair. But we'd never stop. That much we knew as well.

People like me, like us, we exist because of men like Pope. And right or wrong, moral or immoral, I understand why most people would never do the things I've done. Do I blame them? Of course I do. Why wouldn't I? But here's the thing: I blame pieces of shit like Pope more.

It meant what it always meant. It meant what it always will.

We stack his body like wood.

KILLBOX

I look to my hands. My leg. I have been here before. In a different life. At another time. Within a younger memory. I think of my sister. My mother. Each now a ghost decades down the line. I am rage. I am hate. A man who's not only gone further and killed longer than he ever thought possible, but one who knows and has always known there is so much farther to go.

My finger I lose to a degenerate's overbite before I force him to chase the digit in a way not many men have; unclean porcelain that yields to the majority of his skull in time. The bottom part of my right leg is a different story altogether, and one I was fortunate enough to survive. But this final threat, it's one I will not bounce back from, no matter how many chemicals Jeramiah attempts to jam into my veins.

I attach and lock the prosthetic into place. I rise. I move. Watch a body well past its prime walk past a mirror that doesn't hold back. I'm a shell of what I once was. A husk. Sixty pounds shy of what used to fill out the Kevlar for years. Am I being honest? Sure I am. If I've ever been anything, it's a glutton for the truth—self-serving or otherwise.

My hair has left the building as well. Replaced in places by the same ash-coloured stubble that rides my face. A nose now broken more times than I care to remember.

I shower, dress, and attempt to eat. Putting back the milk, I hear Jeramiah pull up, park, and then exit his vehicle. Gravel comes next, becoming louder with each footfall that is his approach.

Good. It was time to begin.

The warehouse's overhead lights flicker as they're turned on, the momentary buzz sounding as the current takes hold.

"I see," Jeramiah says, and he means it in more ways than one. I told him I'd been busy this last little bit. Taking the time I have left and using it the only way I felt I could. "I learned long ago to put nothing past you," he continues, and we move further into the warehouse. "You tell me you think this is the way to go, it's the way to go. Been with you too long to think differently." He wasn't wrong, and as what I'd constructed comes fully into view, I think of Ray and how that man could build. I'd never come close to that man's imagination, no, but then again, I didn't need to. Especially here, now that we'd come to the end.

"Lot of years since anyone used any of those." Jeramiah wasn't wrong here either, the backhoe, steamroller, and cement mixer creating prehistoric shapes from beneath the tarps on our right. "A lot of years indeed," I say, finding myself looking from one polished spot to another across the acreage of floor. Was a time we'd dig up that concrete to dimensions and replace it with new cement. We'd add a human or two as well, and sometimes it would net us a name, sometimes not. Either way, only their heads remained once we got to the end of things, and then just a stub of bone after that.

We move on. Me slower than normal, Jeramiah on my left. Approaching it, Jeramiah slows, turns, and says, "It does what now?"

I smile. Partly because I'm happy, sure, but mostly because now more than ever I knew I would live beyond the grave. Not forever, no, but for a little while at least.

I put one hand on Jeramiah's shoulder. Time to finish the work.

* * *

It's a killbox writ large. My version of one anyway. "One way in," I say. "Zero ways out." Not as rectangular as a shipping container, it resembles one all the same. All white, my goal for it was to house more dirtbags than it currently did.

"Someone's already inside?"

"Come on, let's go over how it works."

I explain my plan and how Jeramiah would have to do most of the heavy lifting—that if he got the word out that I was dead or dying, human garbage would follow. "Who knows," I say, "maybe they even try to eat one another like Joe here." He looks to me, then back to the bank of panels. Three screens in a row, the fibre optics recording from three different angles and at this very moment relaying Joe Scipione and how he remained passed out in a small, congealed puddle of his own blood.

"You given further thought to yesterday's discussion, Joe?" The emaciated man stirs and tries hard to right himself. Dark strands of unwashed hair fall into his face. He attempts to remove these strands with hands that hold half the fingers they used to. Granted he'd gone from smallest to largest, but still, it was far from an unpleasant sight to behold.

"Joe here, he was part of that men's group from a while back. He may or may not have missed that particular meeting I may or may not have attended."

Jeramiah smiles, then utters a *fuck yeah, I knew that was you*, but then I do what I needed to. What I had to.

"Sit," I say, and we both do. "There is nothing after this. You do this or you don't, I can thank you no other way but by saying it. I don't expect you to carry on. I don't expect you to continue to do what we've done." True. All of it. Would I like him to carry on? Sure. I mean, dirtbags choose to be dirtbags every moment of every day. Somebody needs to step up. But the cross I'd chosen to bear, it has never been anyone's but mine. Not Batista's. Not Ray's. And certainly not Jeramiah's. Even then, even if he did choose door number two, I'd want it to be of his own volition and not the obligation he's always seen it as.

"You say that like you already see this as over." Man had me there. It's probably why I look to my hands again. And then to my leg.

"Not quite, no," I say, "but soon."

"Let's say we watch this man eat himself a little bit more, then."

I nod and give him the go-ahead. But as he speaks into the mic, his hand around its base, his face lighting up in ways I have never not understood, I leave him to it and head back to the van. I hear snippets as I leave, however, a *Joe Scipione…listen up.* Then: *I have a story I think you need to hear. You ever hear of a man named Bishop Rider…*

I go on. As does Jeramiah. Not quite like Batista would have, no, but awfully damn close. I hear comparisons next, ones that consisted of bodies and wood, of demons and chases, and finally, of people and how they would burn.

Am I smiling as I reach the door? You're goddamn right I am.

The work, it was being done

ACKNOWLEDGMENTS

I may not have realized it at the start. I may have done it out of sequence. And it may have taken five books for me to do so, but Rider's story, his war, has come to an end. Also, I freely admit killing him in book three IS a weird way to tell a man's story. Either way, the story is his and his story is mine. As well, I have numerous people who helped me on this journey. My wife for one, and even though she's not a reader, she supports me regardless. My kids, all three of you: my greatest accomplishment is getting to be your father everyday. Everyone who took the time to take a early peek and blurb this book. In no particular order, they are: Shannon Kirk, Angel Luis Colon, Steve Weddle, Curtis Ippolito, Zachary Ashford, Manny Torres, Michael Patrick Hicks, Nikki Dolson, Gabino Iglesias, Wayne Fenlon and Shawn Cosby. There is also my Discord group (long live the 'Cord!) and too many to name in the writing community who have supported me and what I've attempted to do through my books. I can't forget Lance Wright either, nor Eric Campbell, the two men I know best at Down and Out Books. And then there's you, dear reader. Rider has some ardent fans. I want you to know I realize this. I also would like you to know that he'd save if he could, saving you the only way he knows how. It's how he was built. It's why he was created. Our own world, it has too many of the things Rider takes apart. I wish it wasn't this way, but it is, and these books, they're really my way of combatting something which should never be. From my heart to yours, thank you for joining me on this ride.

P.S. It takes a village, and it always will. If you dug this book, or any books of mine for that matter, drop a review on either Amazon or Goodreads if you can. I offer you my thanks here, but if I see you on the streets or in my dreams, I'll be sure to thank you there too. See you when I see you,

Beau
August 10, 2022

BEAU JOHNSON lives in Canada with his wife and three boys. He has been published before, usually on the darker side of town. Such fine establishments might include Out of the Gutter Online, Spelk Fiction, Shotgun Honey and the Molotov Cocktail. Besides writing, Beau enjoys golfing, pushing off Boats and certain Giant Tigers.

On the following pages are a few
more great titles from the
Down & Out Books publishing family.

For a complete list of books and to
sign up for our newsletter,
go to DownAndOutBooks.com.

Snake Slayer
Rob Pierce

Down & Out Books
August 2022
978-1-64396-271-9

Three criminals on the run, not just from the law but from other criminals. Two of them are lovers, the third her former lover. Where does love lie, except in the grave?

If you liked Pierce's *Vern in the Heat*, you're going to love *Snake Slayer*. And if you didn't read that one, strap in for the ride.

The Vegas Knockout
A Duffy Dombrowski Mystery
Tom Schreck

Down & Out Books
September 2022
978-1-64396-285-6

Duffy Dombrowski just accepted a dream job: chief sparring partner for Russian heavyweight contender Boris Rusakov in Vegas.

His obstinate basset hound, Al, and a few friends join Duffy for the ride—but before Duffy knows it, his trip turns into a nightmare. Someone's killing local Mexican workers, friends and relatives of Duffy's gym buddies.

And to make matters worse, Duffy's got Boris's Russian mobster pals chasing him with murder on their minds.

Beneath the Black Palms
Stories by Nolan Knight

Down & Out Books
September 2022
978-1-64396-273-3

Come for the sunshine, stay for the dread.

Nolan Knight's masterful, stylistically-diverse short stories expose the nerves of lonesome dreamers, outcasts, squares, con men and have-nots. No one is spared *Beneath the Black Palms*, the most unforgettable short story collection in recent years.

Rock, Roll, and Ruin
A Triangle Sisters in Crime Anthology
Karen Pullen, editor

Down & Out Books
October 2022
978-1-64396-274-0

These twenty-seven stories reflect music in all its forms—from church choir to opera, country to tribal drums.

Of course, rock & roll, the soundtrack of teen lives, predominates—in fiction about Elvis fans, record albums, and bad-boy bands.

Unique stories feature crimes ranging from theft to baby-stealing to murder, each accompanied by a soundtrack, goose bumps, and adrenaline.

CPSIA information can be obtained
at www.ICGtesting.com
Printed in the USA
BVHW040855161022
649471BV00039B/645